Kingdom Principles

Of Financial Increase

Kingdom Principles

Of Financial Increase

by

Dr. Nasir K. Siddiki

Kingdom Principles of Financial Increase
by Dr. Nasir K. Siddiki
ISBN 0-9-666779-0-0

Cover Design: Greg Lane

Editorial Staff: Cynthia Hansen & Jessica Thomas

www.wisdomministries.org

Dedication

I dedicate this book to my three sons, Aaron, Matthew, and Josiah. All three have grown up in a home where Mom and Dad have applied God's kingdom principles of increase as a daily way of life. My heartfelt desire is that as my sons grow to maturity, they would also apply these same principles to their lives in honor of God and His Word.

Certainly I desire that the principles contained in this book would help every person who reads it achieve an abundant, prosperous life. But to my three sons, I say this:

"Aaron, Matthew, and Josiah, there is no one for whom I desire that more than for you. Be faithful to keep God foremost in your lives. Embrace His kingdom principles, and you will experience the faithfulness of your Heavenly Father as you pursue your own God-given path in life."

Contents

Contents

Acknowledgements

First, I want to thank my wife Anita for her constant, loving support through the years. Anita's godly example of giving first inspired me to "live to give." Also, the long hours that Anita spent poring over the manuscript of this book were invaluable in bringing it to its highest level possible.

I want to thank Pastor Mauro Girgenti, whose wise counsel helped point me in the right direction on my quest to discover God's will regarding prosperity.

My thanks to Cynthia Hansen for her diligent work compiling and editing the material for this book and to Jessica Thomas for her final editing.

I also want to thank all the Wisdom Ministries staff and volunteers who worked many hours on this book project to help make it possible! You do not go unappreciated.

Last, but not least a special thank you to Kimberly Hjelt, Melanie Hemry and Gina Jennings for your suggestions and support.

Foreword

Money is a tool, a trial and a test. If you want to expose a man's true character, give him access to large sums of money. Money reveals the heart of a man and the quality of his character. The great king Solomon said, "Money answers all things." In essence, money explains everything. The poor want it. The rich hoard it. It will control these who do not control it, and destroys those who love it. Yet it is necessary for life and required for living effectively. The average man works for it, but the wise man makes it work for him. The subject of money is almost a taboo, especially for the religious, yet the bible speaks more of money than prayer and fasting.

Having the correct understanding and appreciation for this very illusive component of life is critical and must be based on biblical principles. In *Kingdom Principles of Financial Increase,* Dr. Nasir Siddiki presents one of the most profound, yet simple approaches to this essential subject. His logical, yet deeply spiritual presentation of these biblical principles for financial management, giving and receiving, provide a balanced view of a much misunderstood topic. I encourage anyone who wants to have a fundamental perspective of the issue of finances to peel the wisdom from these pages and experience the fruitful life and prosperity that result from applying these time-tested precepts of God.

Dr. Myles Munroe
President: BFM International
Nassau, Bahamas

I was first introduced to Dr. Nasir Siddiki's ministry as I listened to him speak on a Christian television program. Intrigued by his open, friendly manner and obvious knowledge of the Word, I wrote his ministry, asking for some of his teaching tapes. I found that Dr. Siddiki's method of teaching consistently conveys a depth of scriptural knowledge combined with humility, integrity, and godly confidence.

Impressed with Dr. Siddiki's unique and vital teaching on financial increase, I asked him to teach a concentrated, accredited course on Biblical Economics at the American Bible College and Seminary, of which I am the Chancellor. The course was a huge success. It was so well received by the students and faculty alike that Dr. Siddiki was asked to write a book to use as curriculum in the course. The result is this book you hold in your hand.

In May 1998, we at American Bible College and Seminary were pleased to honor Dr. Siddiki for his work in the field of biblical economics by presenting him with an honorary doctorate. We look forward to having him back in the future to teach the Biblical Economics course at our college whenever possible.

I believe you'll find Dr. Siddiki's presentation of God's principles of financial increase both refreshing and life- changing. Dr. Siddiki has achieved a high standard of excellence in both business and ministry. That level of excellence plus the fruit of his search for biblical answers regarding this subject have made him amply equipped to teach you how to live a life of prosperity and success!

W. R. Corvin, Ph.D.
Co-founder and Chancellor
American Bible College and Seminary
Bethany, Oklahoma

Introduction

God has chosen this generation as the runners of the last leg of His great spiritual relay race. The heroes of faith who came before us are even now watching from heaven's grandstands, cheering us on (Hebrews 12:1).

Those godly men and women did their part, and now they have passed the baton to us. It's up to us to accomplish what God has called us to do in these last days and to finish the race. However, that will only be possible if we learn to succeed financially.

I believe that's why God is raising up teachers in the body of Christ. Years ago the Lord told me, "I am going to use your ministry specifically in the area of finances. As you teach My Word line upon line and precept upon precept, the anointing in the Word will go forth to break every yoke of financial bondage. Teach My people, and I will use them as channels through which to funnel millions of dollars into the Gospel."

So in order to fulfill God's divine commission on my life, I travel thousands of miles every year, visiting churches and teaching the principles of financial increase I've set forth in this book. Everywhere my team and I go, God confirms His Word, as incredible financial miracles take place among the church members. For instance, one church experienced a

300-percent increase in income within the first fourteen days after we held a Financial Increase Seminar there!

The truth is, financial miracles are beginning to explode throughout the body of Christ. You may ask, "But why isn't that kind of financial breakthrough happening in *my* life?"

That's the question I want to answer for you. God wants to perform financial miracles in your life as well, and He is capable of doing infinitely more than you can ask, think, or dream (Ephesians 3:20). And not only is He capable, He also *desires* to perform those miracles for you.

Sometimes we limit God by how little we believe Him for, and if we settle for less than His best, then less is all He can do.

I'm going to do all I can to convince you not to settle for less. Let's go after God's highest and best in the realm of prosperity!

The first step in discovering God's best is to focus on what He says in His Word about financial increase. We know that the focused light of a laser beam can cut through steel. In the same way, the focused light of God's truth can cut through all our old ways of thinking and the yokes of bondage that have kept us in poverty and lack for so long.

You can't just read about God's principles of increase and expect anything to change in your financial situation. You have to *do* what God says in His Word to do.

Suppose you are sick and you go to a doctor. The doctor might say, "I'm going to write you a prescription. Take two tablets every four hours for ten days until the prescription is finished."

Will you do what the doctor has asked you to do? Of course, you will. And you won't take four tablets every five hours either. Because you respect the doctor's expert knowledge and want to get well, you are diligent to follow the doctor's exact instructions.

Similarly, if you want your financial situation to change, you need to be just as diligent to learn God's principles for financial increase and apply them to your life. As you do, His spiritual laws regarding finances will become so deeply ingrained on the inside of you that they will ultimately govern the way you think, what you say, and how you act. And you will operate in these godly principles of prosperity as a way of life.

So if you're sick and tired of living in poverty and lack, put your "expecter" on! Get ready to receive revelation from God's Word that will change the way you think, speak, and act in the realm of finances. And as "revelation brings revolution," the focused light of God's truth will break the curse of poverty over your life for good!

Chapter 1
Prosperity—God's Will for You

"Therefore do not be vague and thoughtless and foolish, but understanding and firmly grasping what the will of the Lord is."

—Ephesians 5:17

Is it God's will for you and me to prosper while on this earth? Absolutely yes!

That statement may seem bold, but I'm going to back it up soundly with God's Word. I want to teach you God's principles of financial increase so you can understand and *firmly grasp* what the will of the Lord is about prosperity.

Firmly Grasp the Will of God

You see, if you want to become financially successful, the first step is to firmly grasp that it *is* God's will for you to prosper. Once you know that truth in your heart and grab hold of it in faith, nothing can shake your confidence that prosperity is yours to claim!

For too long the church has told people, "Well, you know, God is a mysterious God who does things in mysterious ways, so no one can ever really know His will."

I beg to differ with that statement. Why would Paul tell the Ephesian church in essence, "You need to make it your business to discover the will of God" if it were impossible to do it? He wouldn't! Paul was basically saying, "Beloved brothers and sisters, God's will isn't supposed to be a hidden, mysterious thing."

It *is* possible to know God's will, because God put His will in His Word. Therefore, we can know God's will. In fact, Paul wrote, **"Awake, you who sleep, arise from the dead, and Christ will give you light"** (Ephesians 5:14 NKJV). The entrance of God's Word brings light and reveals the knowledge of His will.

Of course, at certain times in our lives we have to seek God in prayer to find out His will in a particular matter. We may have to pray, "Lord, please tell me specifically which job to take," or "Lord, which house should I buy?"

But there are other matters we don't have to pray about because God already revealed His will on those subjects in His Word.

For example, we don't have to pray to find out whether or not we should be saved. We know from God's Word that Jesus died on the Cross for every man, woman, and child on this planet and that salvation is God's will (2 Peter 3:9). Therefore, we don't have to go before the Father and say, "If it be Your will, I want to be saved."

If you're born again, you probably don't get up every morning and quote Romans 10:9 ten times for salvation: **"That if thou shalt confess with thy mouth the Lord Jesus, and shalt believe in thine heart that God hath raised him from the dead, thou shalt be saved"** (KJV).

More than likely, the truth of that Scripture is already so alive in your spirit that if I talked to you for hours trying to convince you that you're not saved, you still wouldn't believe me!

That's how firmly you must grasp every one of God's blessings in your life—including prosperity.

Thy Will Be Done on Earth

You can see a particular phrase in the Lord's Prayer in a whole new light once you realize prosperity is God's will for His people. Jesus taught His disciples the Lord's Prayer before He went to the Cross as a guideline on how to pray.

Jesus starts by saying, **"Our Father which art in heaven, Hallowed be thy name. Thy kingdom come. THY WILL BE DONE IN EARTH, AS IT IS IN HEAVEN"** (Matthew 6:9,10 KJV).

So many Christians pray this all the time and don't realize what they're saying! They pray, "God, we want Your will to be done. Whatever is going on up there in heaven, we want it down here on earth."

If you and I want God's will to be fulfilled on earth as it is in heaven, then we must find out what His will is *in heaven*. Consider something. How many people suffer lack in heaven? How many can't pay their bills in heaven? How many file bankruptcy in heaven?

None. Zero. There are no collection agencies in heaven. No one is going to foreclose on the mansion Jesus prepared for you because you didn't make your payment. There is absolutely *no* lack in heaven.

Remember, Jesus said, **"Thy will be done in earth, AS IT IS IN HEAVEN"** (Matthew 6:10 KJV). So if it's not God's will for people to live in poverty and lack in heaven, it can't be His will for people to live that way on this earth either.

In fact, I'll go one step further and say this: If you aren't prospering financially, you are out of the will of God.

The knowledge that it's God's will for you to prosper must become so strong on the inside of you that the moment you begin to experience lack, you refuse to accept it because you *know* it isn't from God. Instead, your first reaction should be to confess in faith, "God takes pleasure in my prosperity. He wants me to be successful and prosperous. He has given me abundant life. So according to God's will, I believe I receive abundant provision for my every need!"

In fact, this kind of attitude pleases God.

God Takes Pleasure in Our Prosperity

Throughout the Bible, God makes it clear that He wants you to prosper. I'll even go so far as to say this: When you're not prospering financially, you're not making God happy. How do I know that? The Bible says so!

> **Let them shout for joy, and be glad, that favour my righteous cause: yea, let them say continually, Let the Lord be magnified, WHICH HATH PLEASURE IN THE PROSPERITY OF HIS SERVANT.**
> —Psalm 35:27 KJV

Notice that this verse *doesn't* say "Let the Lord be magnified, who takes pleasure in His servants barely making it as they live from paycheck to paycheck"! No, it says God takes pleasure in the *prosperity*—not the *poverty*—of His servants.

And if God takes pleasure in the prosperity of His servants, how much more does He take pleasure in the prosperity of His sons and daughters? You see, under the New

Covenant, we are no longer simply God's servants; we are His children, and He wants us blessed!

God purchased us with the blood of His own Son. He adopted us into His family, and He wants us to live a life of abundance.

We as parents want to see our children do well and be abundantly blessed. It grieves us when our children struggle and go through hard times. So it shouldn't surprise us to find out that God feels the same way about *His* children. We're certainly not better parents than He is!

God is a good Father; He doesn't find any joy in seeing His children live on Barely-Make-It Street. He doesn't derive any pleasure from watching them struggle financially all of their lives. What makes God happy and gives Him joy, fulfillment, and excitement is to see His children prosper.

In fact, Jesus said:

If ye then, being evil, know how to give good gifts unto your children, how much more shall your Father which is in heaven give good things to them that ask him?

—Matthew 7:11 (KJV)

Yet people blame God all the time when they're broke. They say, "Look at what God is doing to me. He is making me go through this trial of poverty and lack to teach me how to be humble."

But you won't find one Scripture to prove that point of view. In fact, Second Timothy 3:16 says that God uses *His Word,* not poverty, to reprove, correct, and train us.

Now if you tell me that you're broke because you haven't taken the time to pray or study God's Word, I can accept that explanation. But don't ever say that God is the One keeping you in lack, because then you're actually claiming to be a better parent than He is!

You may ask, "Well, why am I broke if it gives God pleasure to see me prosper? Why doesn't He just go ahead and please Himself by taking care of my needs?"

But it's not up to God whether or not you prosper. It's up to *you*. God already took care of every one of your needs when He sent His Son to die on the Cross. Jesus purchased your right to claim whatever you need in His Word.

So just take a deep breath, relax, and stick with what the Bible says—that God actually finds joy in seeing you prosper!

God's Will—Abundant Life

Let's look at a few more Scriptures which establish beyond a shadow of a doubt that it is God's will for you to prosper in every area of your life. If you have any doubts in the matter, you won't strive for God's best. You'll stay in His permissive will, not His perfect will, for your life (Romans 12:2).

First, let's read what Jesus says about prosperity. Remember, this is our Lord and Savior talking. And when Jesus speaks, we should sit at His feet and hang on every word that comes out of His mouth, because He never wastes His words. John 10:10 says: **"The thief comes only in order that he may steal and may kill and may destroy. I came that they might have and enjoy life, and have it in abundance to the full, till it overflows."**

Jesus says that He came to give us life. That in itself is wonderful, but Jesus didn't stop there. He said, "I'm not satisfied with giving you just a little bit of life. I want to give you life that is overflowing in abundance!"

If Jesus died for you and me so we could have abundant life, I'm not going to settle for anything less. I don't want mediocre life—I want *abundant, filled-to-overflowing* life!

The God of Too Much

The Bible also says that in Christ we are more than conquerors (Romans 8:37). It does *not* say that we're supposed to just get by, barely eking out a living with nothing left over to give to God. That's the opposite of conquering!

Too many Christians today are just getting by. But nowhere in His Word does God say He wants His children to live in lack, because poverty doesn't bring people closer to God.

And we don't serve a God of poverty but a God of abundance. In fact, I'd go so far as to say that we serve a God of *too much!* Malachi 3:10 says He pours out blessings more than you can contain. He created the universe, and everything in it is His. He owns the cattle on a thousand hills (Psalm 50:10). He owns every gold and silver mine on the planet (Psalm 50:12; Haggai 2:8). And He created the vast reservoirs of oil under the ground.

Think back to the story in Genesis of the night God told Abraham to look up at the sky. As Abraham stood gazing at the stars, God said, "I'm going to make you the father of many nations. Go ahead, Abraham, count the stars. That's how many children will come forth from your loins" (Genesis 15:5).

Now God could have made His point to Abraham if only ten thousand stars filled the sky. That alone would have kept Abraham busy counting! But instead, God populated the sky with about one hundred billion galaxies—and each galaxy itself consists of millions of stars. Why did God create such an amazingly vast universe? He did it because He's the God of too much!

Not only is He the God of too much, He is also our *Father*. And when you get the revelation that your Father is the God of too much, all of a sudden you realize that you're linked to a limitless Source.

The revelation of God's abundance should become as strong on the inside of you as the truth of salvation. It should become so deeply ingrained in your heart that if a minister ever preaches a message on "Lack Is Where It's At," you'll immediately respond, "That guy doesn't know his Bible. I *know* the will of God for my life is abundance!"

Three Ingredients:
God, the Word, and You

But now we have a problem to solve. How is it that our Heavenly Father is the God of too much, yet often we are His children of too little? If it is God's will that we live abundantly, why are so many believers out of His will, living in lack? Do we serve El Shaddai (translated "the All-Sufficient One")? Or, as I heard another minister say, do we serve "El Cheapo"?

If we served El Cheapo, then it would be acceptable to be broke. But there's no Scripture to support that possibility. The Bible says we serve El Shaddai, the God who is more than enough.

In fact, the Bible poses this question: If God would give us His Son—His most precious possession—how can we have the audacity to think He would hold back a mortgage payment, college tuition, or any other good thing from us (Romans 8:32)?

People who think God is stingy don't know their God— that His very nature is to give.

So if believers find themselves continually in lack, there is definitely a problem. One time in prayer I asked the Lord, "If You're really the God of abundance, why are so many of Your children struggling? What needs to change in order for Christians to experience the abundant life Jesus talks about in John 10:10?"

The Lord spoke to my spirit and said, "Nasir, there are three ingredients that determine your prosperity.

"Number one is Me, the Father, and I'm here to tell you that I don't change [Malachi 3:6]. I don't bless a few and leave everyone else to suffer lack. I'm the God of love, and My love is for everyone. My mercies are renewed every morning for every person on this earth [Lamentations 3:22,23]. I'm no respecter of persons [Acts 10:34]. I don't have favorites."

"Okay, Lord, I've got it," I said. "You don't change."

"Number two is My Word," the Lord continued. "Now, let Me tell you a little bit about the Word. It doesn't work for one person and not for another. In fact, heaven and earth will pass away, but My Word won't pass away [Matthew 24:35]. My Word is constant; it never changes."

I thought, *Well, this is good. The Lord said there were three ingredients, and the first two are unchanging. If I can just take care of the third ingredient, I'll know the key to prosperity!*

So I asked, "Lord, what's number three?"

"Number three is *you*."

"Me?" I asked in surprise.

"That's right, you."

I didn't want to hear that. None of us want to hear that we are the problem with our finances. We want God to open His heavenly bank account and write us a check!

But if you ever go to your mailbox and find a check signed "God," don't cash it—you'll go to jail. There's not a bank in heaven that issues checks.

Incidentally, all the money you need is on this earth, not in heaven. In fact, all that the body of Christ needs to evangelize the entire world resides right here on this planet.

So I asked the Lord, "Are You telling me that if it were only up to You, we would already possess all the good things You freely supplied out of Your great love for us? Do we suffer lack because of something *we're not* doing?"

"Now you've got it!" the Lord responded.

I thought about it for a moment and then realized I had to humble myself. I said, "Lord, I see it. The problem isn't with You or with Your Word. The problem is with *me*. But I'm willing to change! If You will teach me through the Scriptures what I should do, I will change what I think, say, and do to line up with Your Word."

You see, we all need to humble ourselves before God. The Bible says that the Lord sets Himself against the proud but gives grace, or unmerited favor, to the humble (1 Peter 5:5).

Do you want God's grace and favor operating in your life to prosper you? If you do, you must be willing to change any area of your life that doesn't line up with His Word.

The three ingredients for success—God, the Word, and you—are key to your prosperity. God has provided whatever you need in the Word; however, the Bible that just sits on the bookshelf can't help you. You have to open your Bible and study it. Then you have to *apply* the principles you find there to your life. You have to be willing to change whatever you are doing that is keeping you in lack.

So get this fact settled once and for all: If you're broke, it is not God's fault.

Hunger for God's Word

Another thing I've found out about the secret to prosperity is that *life will give you exactly what you settle for.*

The answer to every problem and struggle in your life—whether sickness, depression, poverty, worry, or oppression—is found in the Word of God. But if you don't hunger and thirst for the Word to find out what it says about your problems, then you'll never find your answer.

The Christian who never hungers or thirsts for the Word struggles along, barely making ends meet all of his life. Then one day he stands before Jesus and says, "Lord, You're my Savior, and I'm so glad to reach heaven. But there's one thing I don't understand. When I was on earth, why was I always struggling because of money?"

The Lord will reply, "The answer is simple. You didn't make it a priority to study My Word. You could have found everything you needed to prosper in My Book."

Now that's sad! But fortunately, it doesn't have to be the case. In fact, I've noticed a spiritual "acceleration" occurring today in the body of Christ. Those who are hungry for the Word are growing spiritually at a more rapid rate than in previous times.

And in the meantime, God keeps telling us to move up even higher in our hunger for the Word. We can't just keep playing church. If we're not willing to get in the Word every day and do what God says, we might as well throw away our Bibles and do something else on Sunday mornings!

The Power in God's Word

Why is it absolutely vital to hunger after God's Word? The Bible says that God watches over His Word to perform it (Jeremiah 1:12). Psalm 119:89 says that His Word is forever settled in heaven, and Psalm 138:2 tells us that God has magnified His Word above His Name.

Get a revelation of the power of God's Word: God exalts His Word even higher than His own Name!

Now the Name of Jesus is powerful. We're told to pray, cast out demons, and lay hands on the sick, all in the Name of Jesus. Why? Because all the power and authority of Almighty God stand behind that Name.

Yet God says His Word is magnified even above His Name. As all-powerful as His Name is, His Word is lifted above it in power. So when God declares that it is His will for you and me to prosper and live an abundant life, we know that promise carries weight!

As we hunger for God's Word, we begin to understand that the mighty power at work in the Word can work *in our lives*. And that's the beginning of biblical prosperity.

Good News to the Poor

We need to catch the spirit of prosperity if we're going to experience financial increase in our lives. What do I mean by "the spirit of prosperity"? It's actually an attribute of the

Spirit-filled life. In other words, one aspect of the Holy Spirit's anointing includes selfless giving.

For example, Jesus explains in Luke 4:18,19 (NIV) that the Spirit of the Lord was upon Him for the primary purpose of giving. In those verses Jesus gives us insight into God's will concerning our prosperity: **"The Spirit of the Lord is on me, because he has anointed me to preach good news to the poor. He has sent me to proclaim freedom for the prisoners and recovery of sight for the blind, to release the oppressed, to proclaim the year of the Lord's favor."**

The Holy Ghost anointed Jesus to give the Good News. In fact, Jesus' entire life consisted of selfless giving.

What good news did Jesus give to prisoners? He proclaims, "You're no longer a prisoner! You can be set free." What good news did He preach to the blind? "You can see again."

And what good news did Jesus give to the poor? "You don't have to stay poor anymore. You can live in abundance!"

Incidentally, that's the only good news the poor want to hear. If you come to them with any other good news, they'll say, "That's all fine, but I'm still broke!" Good news to the poor is *not* "You won't be able to pay your mortgage this month," or "God wants you to stay poor to keep you humble."

But Jesus' message is one of giving. And the same Spirit of God in Jesus lives inside *you* to give as well. Learning to give is essential to catching the spirit of prosperity. The truth is, it ought to be more natural for you to give than to hold back, because the Spirit who lives in you is a giving Spirit.

It's also interesting to note Jesus' first reason for the anointing of God's Spirit: to preach financial increase. I don't believe it's by chance that He put at the top of His list the news that we don't have to be poor anymore.

Why did Jesus give first priority to preaching good news to the poor? For one thing, a person can accomplish a great deal more for the kingdom of God with money than without it. The Gospel is free, but it takes millions of dollars to reach every man, woman, and child with the good news of its life-changing message.

God wants to use His people mightily. He wants to channel large sums of money through them in order to spread the Gospel to the ends of the earth. That's why Jesus preached prosperity to His people!

Was Jesus Poor?

Some people argue, "But Jesus was poor when He walked this earth. He was even born in a manger!"

No, Joseph and Mary only stayed in the Bethlehem stable because all the rooms at the inn were taken—not because they didn't have money. People don't go to a hotel and ask for a room if they don't have the money to pay for it!

Also, remember that the wise men traveled to Bethlehem and gave the infant Jesus gold, frankincense, and myrrh. Later, when Jesus' family escaped to Egypt, they were able to live on the value of those gifts!

"But Jesus didn't even have a place to live," some might suggest. Yet that's not what John 1:38 says. When John the Baptist's disciples asked Jesus, "Where do you live?" Jesus answered, **"Come and see"** (v. 39). Then the disciples spent the day with Jesus where He dwelt.

Someone else might counter, "Jesus was so broke, he had to ride into Jerusalem on a donkey." Are you kidding me? Donkeys were the Cadillacs of Jesus' day. If you had a donkey, you were considered rich!

In actuality, God abundantly supplied Jesus' needs while He walked on this earth. Every time Jesus needed something, He got it. When He needed extra food to feed a multitude, God multiplied a few loaves and fishes (Matthew 14:15-21). When He needed an upper room, the disciples easily secured one for Him (Mark 14:13-16). Jesus even had partners who traveled with Him to take care of His and the disciples' material needs (Mark 15:41).

The Bible also indicates that Jesus' ministry maintained a treasury. We know this from a detail included in John 13:29, which says that when Judas Iscariot abruptly walked out at the Last Supper, the other disciples assumed he was going out to disperse treasury money to the poor, as he had done many times in the past.

Nothing can convince me that Jesus was broke, because He never settled for anything less than God's best during His time on this earth. He even said, "I have come to preach good news to you who are poor—you don't have to settle for poverty any longer!"

Don't Settle for Less Than God's Best

The good news of prosperity continually motivates me to move up higher into the life of abundance God has for me. Many times when I pray, the Lord tells me, "You're thinking too small."

In fact, one time He said, "In all the years you have served Me, I have never been able to give you all I planned for you in any given year. You've limited Me by your level of faith. I am a God of miracles, but if you don't believe Me for them, how can I give them to you?"

When I heard that, I immediately got on my knees and said, "I repent, Lord. I won't settle any longer for less than Your best!"

So stay with the Word until the truth about prosperity explodes on the inside of you. Grasp firmly the will of God and never let it go! Know that Jesus' anointing is to bring abundance into your life, and refuse to settle another day for anything less than God's best for you.

The abundant life Jesus promised isn't for just a select few; it is for every believer. It is for *you*.

Chapter 2
Your Prosperity Is Up to You

**"For all the promises of God in him [Jesus] are yea,
and in him Amen, unto the glory of God by us."**
—2 Corinthians 1:20 (KJV)

Even though your Heavenly Father is the God of too much, He isn't the One who controls how blessed you are in this life—you do. God has already done everything He is ever going to do to provide your abundance. He has given you His Word, and His promises are yea and amen.

Two Sides of God's Promises

But for every promise, there is a man-ward side and a God-ward side to fulfill. If the man-ward side isn't accomplished, the promise will not come to pass.

For instance, Jesus died for all mankind, but not all mankind is saved. To be saved, a person believes in his heart that Jesus rose from the dead and releases his faith with his mouth by confessing Jesus as His Lord and Savior (Romans 10:9).

So if a man cries out, "God, save me!" God the Father asks, "Jesus, what is he talking about?" Jesus replies, "I don't know. I already redeemed him from his sins. I don't have to go back to earth to die on the Cross again, because the price has been paid."

Another man cries out to God, "Help, I need money! My business is folding! I can't pay my rent!" The Father looks over and asks, "Jesus, what do You make of this?" Jesus answers, "I don't know, Father. I already paid the price for his prosperity. I already redeemed him from the curse of poverty with My blood."

You see, the issue is no longer what God can do for us. He has already provided for every need. Just as surely as Jesus died on the Cross so our sins could be forgiven, He also died on the Cross so you and I could be redeemed from the curse of poverty. Now the issue is what you and I must do to be *more* than conquerors.

To Him That Overcometh

Jesus said that experiencing victory in life is our own responsibility: **"To him that overcometh will I grant to sit with me in my throne, even as I also overcame, and am set down with my Father in his throne"** (Revelation 3:21 KJV).

Notice that Jesus never said He would do your overcoming for you; the responsibility lies with you. If you're living a defeated life, in essence it's your own fault.

You may be waiting right now for God to change your situation. But He is saying, "Everything you need to be an overcomer is in My Word! Because I already did My part, now it's your job to do the overcoming."

God won't ask you to do something you can't do. For example, He wouldn't tell you to become a bird, because there is no way you could do it. God will only tell you to be something that you *can* be. So if Jesus said you can be an overcomer, you can!

Not only can you be a conqueror in life, but you can be *more* than a conqueror! You can overcome every yoke that binds you and every symptom of lack that threatens your financial security. You can overcome every one of the devil's strategies to steal, kill, and destroy God's blessings in your life.

But don't fool yourself into thinking you can avoid dealing with the devil's strategies. Jesus wouldn't talk about "him who overcomes" unless you had something to overcome. You can't be more than a conqueror if you have nothing to conquer.

So Jesus lets you know that you *will* face some problems in this life, and He also indicates the changes you may need to undergo in order to overcome those problems.

You see, we do need to change in some situations. One good definition of insanity is "doing the same thing over and over again and expecting different results." So you must think differently, act differently, and speak differently if you want your problems to change.

You don't have to be poor anymore. That's history. You never need to experience poverty again, but it's up to you. You either take God at His Word, or you don't.

So if you experience financial problems, don't wait for Jesus to do your overcoming for you. Humble yourself before God and say, "Lord, what am I doing wrong? Whatever it is, I'm willing to change. Show me what to do differently." That's always your first step to overcoming.

The Prosperous Soul

So our first step is knowing it's up to us to overcome poverty and lack in our lives. But what is the next step we take toward accomplishing that? We find an important key in something the apostle John wrote to believers: **"Beloved, I pray that you may prosper in all things and be in health, just as your soul prospers"** (3 John 2 NKJV).

Now John was a man who spent a lot of time with Jesus. For three years he walked with Jesus, lived with Jesus, and talked with Jesus.

Jesus had many disciples, but He was closer to some than to others. For example, He sent out seventy disciples, but only twelve disciples followed Him everywhere He went; and of the twelve, three disciples were closer to Him than the others. Out of those three, one disciple was the closest of all—John the beloved.

So I imagine John knew a little bit about the will of God! And in this verse John is praying according to God's divine will under the direction of the Holy Spirit.

What then does John mean here? **"Beloved, I pray that you may prosper in all things...."** One of the meanings of the word *prosper* is a progression or a journey.

God wants us to keep moving forward moment by moment, year by year out of our limitations. In any area of life, if we're not in a better place today than we were six months ago, then we're not prospering in that area.

Notice John doesn't say we are to prosper or progress in two or three areas only. No, we are to prosper in *all* areas of our lives—physically, mentally, emotionally, spiritually, *and* financially.

You see, prosperity is not just an abundant supply of money, although it does include that. But many in the world possess great riches and still don't find happiness. True prosperity is success in every area of life, including finding happiness.

But then John offers the condition: **"...prosper... and be in health, JUST AS YOUR SOUL PROSPERS."** That's talking about the measure of God's Word that you're actually living—*not* just the number of Scriptures you know.

If your soul isn't prospering, don't expect your pocketbook to prosper. You see, if you become financially prosperous without developing corresponding soulish prosperity, you may eventually lose your wealth because you may not understand the spiritual laws and principles that affect the financial realm.

I know that because it happened to me. Years ago I was a millionaire, but the time came when I lost my wealth in just a few months! Why? Because at the time my soul had not prospered proportionately to the finances I had acquired.

Sometimes even the enemy will bring you wealth to cause you to change your focus from God to mammon, or the love of money. Jesus was talking about that change in focus when He said you can't serve two masters—God *and* money (Luke 16:13).

God wants to make sure you *don't* change your focus as you become prosperous. Therefore, it's His will that the prosperity in your pocketbook grows in proportion to the prosperity in your soul.

Man in Three Parts:
Spirit, Soul, and Body

In order to learn how the soul is to prosper in proportion to our finances, it's important to understand the three parts of man: spirit, soul, and body.

Remember, I said there is a man-ward side and a God-ward side to every promise of God. Until we fulfill the man-ward side, we won't see the God-ward part of the promise manifested in our lives. But if we do our part, God does His.

So what is the man-ward part according to Third John 2? How do you make your soul prosper? To answer those questions according to the Word of God, you first must understand the three-part nature of man. First Thessalonians 5:23 says, **"May your SPIRIT and SOUL and BODY be preserved sound and complete [and found] blameless at the coming of our Lord Jesus Christ, the Messiah."**

This Scripture indicates we are spirit beings who live in a physical body and have a soul. The body is nothing more than the outward clothing we wear during this earthly life. One day our bodies will decay—unless of course we are caught away first in the rapture and receive our incorruptible bodies.

So your body isn't you; it's something you live in. Your soul isn't you either, although it includes your mind, emotions, and will. The soul is something you possess, not something you *are*.

You see, the Bible says that God created man in His own image (Genesis 1:26). God is Spirit (John 4:23,24), so if He created us in His image, then we also are spirit beings. Consequently, your spirit, created in the likeness of God, is the real you. When you were born again, only your spirit was recreated—your mind and body were not changed. The Holy Spirit dwells within your spirit, not your soul or body.

That's why Romans 12:1 says that *you*—your spirit man—must present your body to God. Your spirit, the real you, must control your body by presenting it to God as a living sacrifice.

Renew Your Mind by the Word

For too long we've allowed our bodies to dominate us, telling us what to do and when to do it. So how do we both take control of our bodies and cause our souls to prosper? We do it by renewing our minds according to Romans 12:2: **"Do not be conformed to this world—this age, fashioned after and adapted to its external, superficial customs. But be transformed (changed) by the [entire] renewal of your mind—by its new ideals and its new attitude—so that you may prove [for yourselves] what is the good and acceptable and perfect will of God, even the thing which is good and acceptable and perfect [in His sight for you]"**.

To be in the perfect will of God, you must learn to dominate your body through the renewing of your mind. Renewing your mind is essential because unless you do, you won't perceive what God's will is! And how can your soul prosper when you're not walking in the light of God's perfect will?

God wants us to follow the leading of His Spirit in every decision we make. That's how our souls will prosper. But we can only know His will in every situation of life as we change the way we think, conforming our thoughts to the Word of God.

You see, *revelation must cause a revolution*. You have not truly received revelation from God's Word unless it has caused a revolution in the way you think, act, and speak.

No matter how you were raised, the Word of God should completely determine your thought life—not experience or circumstances. You must think in line with God's Word in order to cause your soul to prosper.

But your mind doesn't automatically get renewed. Instead, you allow it to be changed by the power in God's Word, by your own will casting down thoughts and imaginations that exalt themselves against the knowledge of God (2 Corinthians 10:3-5).

God doesn't change the way you think; *you* have to do it. That just doesn't happen by listening to one sermon on Sunday morning, but by getting into the Word every day for yourself.

You know, Christians eat two or three times a day because they want their physical bodies to stay strong and healthy. Yet too often they starve their spirit man who lives inside their physical bodies by trying to get by on one cold snack on Sunday morning. But if they tried to feed their bodies like that, their bodies would disown them!

That's why so many believers continue to think the same way they did before they got saved. They haven't renewed their minds, and, therefore, they make wrong decisions which adversely affect their souls' prospering.

People with unrenewed minds may have been saved forty years, but spiritually, they may only be about four years old. You see, a person's spiritual age isn't based on how long he's been born again but on how many years he's been feeding his spirit man with the Word.

Actually, a regular diet of the Word is even more important than the natural food you eat. The Holy Spirit is your Teacher and Guide, and He desires to direct you in every move in life. But He has a tough job when there is very little Word in your heart to bring to your remembrance. His ability to guide you into prosperity in every area of life depends on your diligence to renew your mind by feeding on God's Word.

If you limit feeding your spirit to Sunday mornings, you will never be an overcomer and never go from victory to victory. You will never experience the abundant life Jesus came to give you.

Until you get serious and commit yourself to renewing your mind with the Word, you'll be just like the average Christian who might say, "I can quote lots of Scriptures, but don't ask me to live them!"

Jesus doesn't really care how many Scriptures you can quote. What matters to Him is how many you actually *live*.

The only way you can walk in the light of the truth you know regarding financial increase and your soul's prospering is to change the way you think. And there is only one way you can do that—by renewing your mind with the Word of God.

It bothers me when I see Christians running out to buy how-to books about financial success which aren't scriptural. I haven't found one Scripture that says you can renew your mind by reading about the habits of successful people!

God says there is only one way to renew your mind: delve hungrily into the Word and it will cause your soul to prosper.

The Deciding Vote

With every daily decision, the three parts of our nature, spirit, soul, and body, conduct a voting process on the inside of us.

Now the simple formula for success is this: Learn to make every decision the right one. When we make right decisions—to go to the right school, marry the right person, get the right job, start the right business at the right time—it's easy to succeed. The problem is, too often we make *wrong* decisions, and we don't even know why.

So in order to be successful in life—to prosper just as our souls prosper—we have to know how this decision process works on the inside of us. Here's what happens. In any given situation, the spirit man says, "I want to do this in line with the Word."

But the flesh says, "No, I want to do it *my* way!"

Then there is the soul or mind. Whichever way the mind votes determines the outcome of the decision, because the third vote creates a majority.

If your mind decides, "I want to go with how my body feels," then you will make your decisions based on what your flesh and mind have decided and you won't walk in the realm of the Spirit. That's precisely what has happened with every bad decision you've made since you became born again.

If you don't renew your mind, it will always side in with the flesh and you'll go from failure to failure, never experiencing the victory God has for you. But as you allow the Word to change your way of thinking, more and more your mind will begin to cast a vote with your spirit in the decisions of life. And the Holy Spirit dwelling in your spirit will direct you according to God's perfect will.

You see, your financial success is not determined by your circumstances but by your *response* to circumstances. In a sense, it doesn't matter what is going on around you—you can still succeed. It makes no difference whether or not your pocketbook or bank account is empty; you can still become prosperous.

What I mean is simply this. If you respond to decisions according to the flesh, you will remain in the natural realm, where circumstances can defeat you. But if you will renew your mind with God's Word in order to respond according to the ways of the Spirit, you will always triumph over the circumstances of life as an overcomer.

Let me give you an example of what I'm talking about. Say you're in a restaurant and you've had a wonderful meal. You're completely full and can't eat another bite. But when the waitress comes with the dessert menu, she says, "Today we have fresh, moist, succulent, mouth-watering cheesecake."

You look at the picture of the cheesecake and start to drool. You love cheesecake! Your flesh says, "I want it! I want it! Give me that cheesecake. I must have it!"

But your spirit man says, "You don't need that cheesecake. You're supposed to present your body as a living sacrifice, so time out! You've eaten enough."

Your flesh protests, "But I love cheesecake. I want cheesecake. I have to get some cheesecake!"

That's when the mind determines the deciding vote—cheesecake or no cheesecake. An unrenewed mind might suddenly think, *Hey, I know! I'll just order a diet Coke instead of a regular one, and then I'll have the cheesecake!*

That may seem like a trivial example, but the truth is, you and I stand at the crossroads of a decision every day of

our lives. How we respond each day to the big and little decisions we face determines both our soulish and financial prosperity—and ultimately our success in every realm of life.

Making Right Decisions
With Your Finances

We've just seen that the level of our financial prosperity
is in direct proportion to our level of diligence in renewing
our minds with God's Word. Now let's look specifically at
examples of how our minds determine our response in financial situations.

When it's time for the offering at church, your flesh may
say, "Hey, I don't have enough for myself and the bills this
month. I can't afford to give!" But the spirit man responds,
"I'm short on finances because I haven't planted enough seed.
I'd better give in this offering!"

The mind wonders, "Well, which should I side with?" If
your mind is not renewed with the Word of God, it will probably side with the flesh and the money will stay in your wallet.

But when you line up your mind with the Word, you'll follow your spirit and make the right decisions in your giving
and in your business dealings.

When making business decisions, your spirit says, "I
want to choose integrity," while your flesh argues, "But I
want to do whatever is necessary to make the highest profit."
Then your renewed mind makes the deciding vote: "I will do
what is just and fair for the other guy, because the Word
teaches that I will always reap what I sow."

Imagine if all businessmen did what was right, just, and
fair! They would put lawyers out of business, because there
would be no need to sue anyone.

When you get a revelation that your financial success totally pivots on the renewal of your mind, you'll study the Word daily! It's the most important step you will take on the road to prosperity. It's the man-ward side to fulfilling God's promises in your life.

So feed on the Word, renew your mind, and change your thinking. Refuse to let anything keep you from the Word of God, because only the Word will change your life and help you walk in God's victory for you. God has given you everything you need to prosper—now your prosperity is up to you!

Chapter 3
Power and Purpose To Get Wealth

"But you shall (earnestly) remember the Lord your God; for it is He WHO GIVES YOU POWER TO GET WEALTH, that He may establish His covenant which He swore to your fathers, as at this day."
—Deuteronomy 8:18

We've already seen from God's Word that He takes pleasure in seeing us prosper in life. But as we've just discovered, prosperity is up to us. In other words, God isn't the One who gives us wealth! God didn't say in that verse, "It is I who gives you wealth." He said, "I give *you* power to get wealth."

God is in the Power-Giving Business

A lot of people mistakenly seek God for wealth. They beg Him, "Lord, give me money! give me money!" never realizing that God isn't in the *money*-giving business. He has no bank in heaven, and He's not waiting to throw a moneybag down from the sky. No, God is in the *power*-giving business.

The Hebrew word for *power* in Deuteronomy can be translated as *forces*, *abilities*, and *fruits*. In other words, God has given us laws and principles that have the force or ability behind them to produce the fruit of wealth. It's up to us to simply find out what those principles are and then to walk in them.

After all, since God is in the power-*giving* business, it stands to reason that you and I should be in the power-*seeking* business, seeking God for the power to increase financially by studying the principles of prosperity found in His Word.

You see, God wouldn't say, "I take pleasure in your prosperity, but I won't show you how to prosper." For one thing, that would make Him unhappy! No, God says, "I delight in seeing you prosper, and I'll show you by My Word how to do it."

Notice that one of God's instructions to us is that we earnestly remember Him as the One giving us the power to get wealth. Why does He tell us that? I think it's that when people experience a little success and things are going well in their lives, they tend to forget God. Many actually begin to think their financial increase came as a result of their job, their business, or their own skills instead of by the grace and ability of God.

So when you experience increase, always remember that you didn't do it by yourself; *God* empowers you to prosper.

The Purpose Behind the Power To Get Wealth

God instructed me once, "Don't ever teach on My *principles* of financial increase without teaching on My *purpose* for financial increase."

If we forget God's purpose for giving us power to get wealth, we'll have a real problem applying His principles of prosperity to our lives. That same verse in Deuteronomy tells us the nature of His divine purpose: **"It is He Who gives**

you power to get wealth, THAT HE MAY ESTABLISH HIS COVENANT which He swore to your fathers" (Deuteronomy 8:18*)*.

This verse tells us two things: Number one, if we get wealth but don't establish His covenant, we are out of His will. And number two, if we don't seek to learn His principles of getting wealth for the purpose of establishing His covenant—if we are just content to stay broke—we are again out of His will.

God gives us the ability to produce wealth for one main purpose: to reach out all over the world with the Gospel.

Israel failed to understand that purpose. They were God's chosen people. After possessing the Promised Land, they had wealth in abundance because the land God gave the Israelites was rich and fertile, flowing with milk and honey (Exodus 3:8). Remember, it took two men to carry one enormous bunch of Canaan's grapes on a staff (Numbers 13:23)!

As the Israelites charged forth to possess the land, the power of Almighty God helped them. They didn't even have to knock down the walls of Jericho to fight the inhabitants—the walls collapsed by the power of God as the people followed His instructions (Joshua 6:20).

So the Israelites possessed the Promised Land God gave them, with the understanding that they were to be an example of His covenant to all of their neighboring nations. But the Israelites didn't fulfill what they were called to do. Instead of living in righteousness as God's covenant people, they began to worship their neighbors' idols.

Because the Israelites failed to establish God's covenant on the earth as He had commanded them to do, that failure eventually caused them to go into captivity in Babylon.

Now we don't want to make the same mistake the Israelites did, neglecting what God has commanded us to do. And what has He commanded us? Jesus commissioned us to preach the Gospel throughout the world (Mark 16:15). You see, He didn't die for just one nation or for a chosen few; He died so people of every nation could be saved.

Jesus died because people—*not* money—are the riches of heaven. Gold, silver, and jewels carry no value there. Those substances, which are so precious on this earth, bedeck mere building blocks and pavement in heaven!

We need to value what God values—people. But many Christians don't share God's heart for people. They may say, "I don't need a lot of money, Lord. I'm happy with a little bit. I just want enough for me, my wife, my two kids, and my dog."

That's selfish! Christians with that kind of attitude are out of God's will. They don't realize that you can't take a car, a house, or even a piece of jewelry to heaven with you. The only things you take to heaven are the souls you helped bring into God's kingdom by sharing or funding the Gospel.

Others say, "But if I make millions, I'm afraid I'll be distracted and stop serving God." That's why it's important to fix your heart on serving Him before you ever begin to seek wealth. Change your purpose. Line it up to fit God's purpose.

God has His heart set on one purpose: getting as many children as possible to heaven. He gave His best for that very purpose. Now He's looking for those in His family through whom He can flood millions of dollars to bring multitudes into His kingdom. He wants every man, woman, and child saved.

Six billion people live on this planet, and about five billion of those people still need to hear about Jesus. That's not acceptable to God, nor should it be to us.

The Precious Fruit of the Earth

The time is short. There is a work that needs to be done quickly before Jesus returns, and we're not waiting on Him to do something; He's waiting on *us*. James 5:7 says God waits for the precious fruit of the earth, which comes as every person on this planet has the chance to hear about Him and accept Him as Savior.

I believe something is going to happen very quickly in these last days, that the body of Christ is going to reap a harvest of souls of a magnitude more than we can dream, think, or imagine.

Jesus said that the harvest is ripe (Matthew 9:37), that's not the issue. So what is the issue that's stopping the church from bringing in the harvest? Usually, it's a lack of money.

The Lord once said to me, "The last stronghold of the enemy in the body of Christ is in the area of finances. Many people have given Me their hearts, their heads, and their bodies, but they won't give Me their wallets."

But that stronghold has to be broken! In order for God to prosper us so we can fund the Gospel, we must give Him our wallets as well, because only then can He multiply a return to us. Jesus is coming soon, and there is a harvest of souls to reap. We don't have a lot of time, and therefore, we have to break out of our carnal limitations—those invisible walls that hold us back from fulfilling our role in God's end-time harvest.

This great harvest is going to require a lot of money, because it takes money to send the Gospel around the world. It takes money to build churches and print Bibles.

That's why God is thrusting millions of dollars into the hands of believers. In fact, supernatural miracles in the financial realm are on the increase. For instance, I heard about a minister who received three-and-a-half million dollars in one offering—and only five hundred people were in the service!

Now is also the time for God's transfer of wealth to come to pass according to Proverbs 13:22: **"The wealth of the sinner is laid up for the just"** (KJV). And I believe such a transfer has already begun.

So don't tell me God can't get you the necessary funds. Just line up your purpose with God's purpose, and believe Him for what you need. His covenant guarantees that He'll find a way to get wealth to you. And because you have His heart and motives on the inside of you, you can go to the Father and ask Him for anything you need.

As you begin to prosper financially, never forget your mandate to spread the Gospel to the ends of the earth. If God can get money *through* you to fund the end-time harvest, He will get it *to* you.

So be a river, not a dam. Stretch beyond your own personal needs, and make it your highest priority to establish and share God's covenant with the people of this earth.

God Will Keep His Part Of the Covenant

There is another meaning to the promise that God will give us the power to get wealth. God is also saying to us, "I will give you the principles and abilities you need to produce wealth because that's My side of the bargain. If you choose not to apply those principles or use those abilities, you won't prosper. Nevertheless, I will fulfill My part of the deal by making them available through My covenant."

The covenant God is talking about is the one He made with Abraham. That covenant included three things: Number one, God told Abraham, "I will make you the father of many nations" (Genesis 17:4). We know that promise came to pass with the birth of Abraham's promised son Isaac.

Number two, God said, "I will greatly bless you" (Genesis 12:2). Genesis 13:2 says that Abraham was not just rich but *very* rich.

Number three, God told Abraham, "Not only will I bless you, Abraham, but I will make you a blessing to others" (Genesis 12:2). And God did make Abraham a blessing to others, even to his own nephew Lot.

God cut covenant with Abraham, not with Lot, yet God made Abraham so rich and such a blessing that Lot also prospered because of it. In fact, the two of them couldn't even live in the same area together because they had so many possessions, livestock, and servants (Genesis 13:5-12)!

God fulfilled His part of the covenant once Abraham did what he was supposed to do: believe. And God will do the same for us as we fulfill our part of the covenant. We are to believe God as heirs of the promise God gave to Abraham, who is the father of our faith according to Romans 4:16. God promises to extend the Abrahamic blessing of abundance to us as we follow His principles of increase by faith.

Preparing Your Heart for Prosperity

Let me make it clear that God doesn't mind if you own an abundance of material things; He just doesn't want those things to own *you*. He's looking to the day when you have matured spiritually to the point that you rely completely on Him, not on material gain, because then He can flood finances through you to get His Gospel out to the world. And that time of spiritual maturation prepares your heart to receive prosperity.

One day the Lord said to me, "Nasir, when man looks at man, the first thing he sees is flesh. Then as he gets to know the person, he learns about the person's heart. But I am Spirit. The first thing I see when I look at man is the heart."

You see, preparation for prosperity begins in the heart. It's like the farmer; he doesn't throw his seed carelessly on just any kind of ground and then expect it to grow. No, he carefully prepares the ground, making it as fertile as possible to receive the seed so he can ensure a good harvest.

Similarly, the Bible says your heart is the soil into which the Word of God is sown (Mark 4:14-20). In order for that supernatural seed to take root and grow into abundance, you must prepare your heart, keeping it pure before God.

Too many believers aren't seeing the hundred, sixty, or even thirtyfold return on their giving that the Word tells us we can expect. Why is that? Often it's due to the poor condition of their hearts.

On the other hand, you may look at some prominent ministers of our day and wonder, *Why are their ministries exploding? Why are they experiencing such a huge inflow of finances to help them fulfill their call? I'd be satisfied to receive* any *kind of return on my giving!*

But then God says, "Wait a minute—how many years did those ministers prepare their hearts? How long did it take them to learn how to walk in integrity and purity before they could possess material wealth without that wealth possessing *them*?"

It may have taken twenty, thirty, or forty years before those seasoned ministers saw their ministries financially explode. However, that doesn't mean you have to wait that long before you're prepared for prosperity. By diligently hungering after God's Word, you can tap into the acceleration I believe is taking place in the Spirit in these last days.

The heart preparation that took years in the past will take months now. What took months will take weeks, and what took weeks will take days or hours. But determine daily to keep your heart pure before God and line up your purposes with His purposes so He can do His quick work preparing your heart.

What is Your Motive?

Consider your own heart. What is your motive for increasing in the realm of finances? Is it the motive God has? Remember, God sees the motives of your heart long before He takes a look at the rest of you. The nature of those motives determine whether or not the Heavenly Father can prosper you as He desires.

As a natural father, I deal the same way with my children. For instance, my young son, Matthew, would love to take my car keys, jump in our van, and take it for a ride. But it would definitely not be wise for me to give Matthew my keys and let him drive that van! He would hurt himself.

And no one would accuse me or say, "Nasir, you selfish father, you! You won't even give your son the car keys!" No, I love my son, and that's why I won't give him the car keys.

God the Father loves us the same way. He can't give us great financial increase if we're not mature enough to handle it properly.

Someone once put it to me this way, "Don't ever believe God for $10,000 unless you're prepared to do with that $10,000 what God would do."

It isn't *your* money; you're just a steward. Remember, everything you own belongs to God anyway—in fact, Jesus bought you yourself with His blood! So if you're not willing to do with your increase what God would do, in a sense, you don't have a right to ask Him for it.

What would God do with that $10,000? He would find a way to bring more souls to heaven. That's what His motive and His heart's desire is. But if your heart's desire doesn't line up with His, don't hang around waiting for your finances to increase. If you want His power to produce wealth, be prepared in your heart to obey Him with that wealth.

Let me illustrate. Suppose you worked as the manager in a company I owned and I gave you money with specific instructions about what to do with it. What would happen if you did what you wanted with the money instead of following my instructions? You wouldn't be working for me anymore.

In a similar way, you're working for God in the service of the kingdom. Suppose you pray, "Lord, help me. I need finances!" and the Lord says, "Okay, here's some money." But if you use the money for something other than what He would want you to do with it, not obeying Him with the money you do have, God isn't going to trust you with more.

Too often we're only interested in increasing our lifestyle. That's not a very popular statement, but it's the truth. The bottom line is, we should always ask the Lord, "What do *You* want me to do with this money?"

I encourage you to get God's purpose deep on the inside. Keep your motives pure as you apply God's principles of financial increase. You have been placed on this earth at this time for a reason and a purpose, and you play a vital role in the work to be done, the Gospel to be preached, and the people to be reached.

You may say, "Well, I don't know if God wants to use me in the end-time harvest." Friend, if you are a member of the body of Christ, God wants to use you. I guarantee that when you were saved, God didn't hold a heavenly board meeting with the Son and the Holy Ghost and ask, "What are we going to do with this new addition to Our family? We never planned on that person coming into the kingdom!"

But God didn't save you just so you could sit on a pew either. His calling on your life is to get involved in some way in the end-time harvest.

"But I'm not a preacher or a teacher," you might protest. That may be true, but you *are* still a minister of the Gospel. God has given us all the ministry of reconciliation (2 Corinthians 5:19). That ministry includes giving into God's kingdom for the sake of the Gospel.

So make God's motive for prosperity *your* motive as well. Believe God for increase not only to meet your own personal needs but also to fulfill your role in the end-time harvest of souls!

We Are to Be the Salt Of the Earth

Jesus said in Matthew 5:13 that we are to be the salt of the earth. Salt makes people thirsty, and that's what we as Christians are supposed to do: make people thirsty for God.

But that probably isn't going to happen if you live in poverty and lack all the time! When you tell the world how great your Jesus is and yet you have holes in your shoes, they aren't going to say, "Oh, I want to be broke and poor just like you!" No, people in the world will look at you and say, "Thank you, but no, thank you. I don't want to be like you, so I don't think I want to know your God."

You see, the world is hungry for success. Therefore, the more broke you are, the less people are going to listen to your witness. They've already figured out how to be broke, so they don't need your help with that. But start living as more than a conqueror, with your needs abundantly met and plenty left over to help others, and people will want to know your God!

We Christians have the Greater One living on the inside of us; therefore, we should be the most successful people in the world in every area of life. And if we're not, then something is wrong!

But as we receive revelation from the Word of God and become doers of the Word, we can tap into God's power to produce wealth and become prosperous in every realm of life.

As we seek to establish God's covenant on this earth, we'll witness the turn-around God has planned all along. Instead of struggling along on Barely-Make-It Street all of our defeated lives, we will shine forth as the salt of the earth, God's glorious, victorious church. And that's when the world will start coming to us for the answers it desperately needs!

Chapter 4
Our Key to Prosperity—
Knowledge of God's Word

"And these are the ones by the wayside where the word is sown. And when they hear, Satan comes immediately and takes away the word that was sown in their hearts."

—Mark 4:15 NKJV

Long before you battle financial problems, you must win the battle in the arena of the knowledge of God's Word. The enemy knows that if he can keep you ignorant of God's Word, he will defeat you in every area of life.

The Enemy is After the Word

The enemy not only wants to keep you ignorant of God's Word, but he wants you to stay ignorant of his strategies against you. You see, if you don't understand what the enemy is after in your life, you won't guard it.

One day as I was meditating on some Scriptures, the Lord spoke to me about this. He asked, "Do you know what the enemy is really after?"

"Yes," I replied, "he's after my finances."

"No," the Lord said. "Don't you know that he's the god of this world system? He has all the finances he wants; he doesn't need yours. Your extra twenty dollars isn't going to make or break the devil."

"Well, then, he's after my health or my kids."

"No, he's not even after that."

"Then what *is* the enemy after, Lord?"

"He's after the Word," the Lord answered. "He knows that if he can stop you from renewing your mind with the Word, he doesn't have to defeat you—you're already defeated! Your flesh will take care of that."

What the Lord told me makes sense. Let me show you what that means. The Bible lists our spiritual armor in Ephesians 6:13-17. But have you ever noticed that every piece of armor—the helmet of salvation, breastplate of righteousness, belt of truth, shield of faith, and shoes of peace—is defensive in nature? Only the sword of the Spirit, which is the Word of God, is an offensive weapon.

That's why the devil tries so hard to keep you away from church, teaching tapes, or books that can help you grow spiritually. He also tries to keep you so busy day by day that you never have time to study the Word. Satan's first tactic is always to separate you from your "sword" so you have nothing to attack him with.

The day I first received that revelation, I didn't walk to the Word—I ran! I read books, I listened to tapes, I attended church every time the door was open, and I constantly asked my pastor questions.

I'm telling you, I got *hungry* for the Word! I knew if I could get the Word of God in my heart, I could live a victorious life.

So make sure *you* don't play into the devil's hands by ignorance of the Word. Regularly attend a church that teaches the uncompromised Word of God. Study the Bible daily and plant it deep in your heart, because the Word is your source of victory.

Let me give you another example of how important the Word is to your survival. After fasting for forty days in the wilderness, Jesus Himself won a major victory over the devil because He recognized the importance of using the Word. (Matthew 4:1-4).

When Jesus became hungry, the enemy tempted Him to turn stones into bread. But Jesus said, **"Man shall not live by bread alone, but by every word that proceedeth out of the mouth of God"** (v. 4 KJV).

Jesus understood that we cannot live by bread (or pizza, chicken, or steak!) alone. In other words, feeding upon God's Word is actually more important than eating necessary food. Only as we make it a daily priority to seek God's Word do we put ourselves in a position to triumph over the devil's devices.

The Enemy's Number-One Weapon:
Lack of Knowledge

The Bible tells us what happens when the enemy succeeds in keeping God's people from knowing the Word: **"My people are destroyed for lack of knowledge"** (Hosea 4:6 KJV).

It's interesting to note that the Bible does not say we are destroyed for lack of money or lack of faith. No, the primary weapon the enemy uses against us is lack of knowledge. He knows that if he can hold us back through ignorance, he can destroy us.

You see, long ago God set into motion laws and principles that govern the universe. Whether we know about those laws or not, they nonetheless govern our lives. Lack of knowledge doesn't change the operation of God's laws, but it does keep us from obeying or benefiting from them.

For instance, suppose I were to climb to the top of a three-story building and prepare to jump off. You'd no doubt yell, "Nasir, don't do it! You'll fall and hurt yourself! There is such a thing as the law of gravity, you know."

And what if I yelled back, "I don't believe in that law! I'm going to jump anyway!" Guess what? Whether I believe in gravity or not, I'm going *down* when I jump! I'm going to suffer for my lack of knowledge about the law of gravity.

So whatever area of life you lack knowledge in is the area in which you will suffer. For example, as long as the enemy can separate sinners from the knowledge that Jesus paid the price for their sins, they'll stay unsaved. Likewise, as long as the devil can keep you from knowing it's God's will to prosper you, you'll stay poor. You won't be any threat to the devil in that area because you can't act on what you don't know.

Remember the woman with the issue of blood? (Mark 5:25-34.) She suffered with extreme sickness for twelve years. Despite her seeing many doctors over the years, she only grew worse.

Before this woman could win in the arena of healing, she had to win first over ignorance. Remember, she said, **"If I may touch but his clothes, I shall be whole"** (v. 28 KJV).

The woman must have known something about Jesus as the Healer to speak this way. Then she acted on that knowledge in faith. She went to Jesus believing what she had heard about Him, and she received her healing!

Knowledge Sets the Captive Free

Isaiah 5:13 says something similar to the Scripture we looked at in Hosea: **"Therefore my people are gone into captivity, BECAUSE THEY HAVE NO KNOWLEDGE"** (KJV).

Their own lack of knowledge holds God's people captive. But Jesus said knowledge of God's truth sets people free (John 8:32)!

That verse in Isaiah reminds me of a true World War II account I once heard. During the war, Japanese soldiers invaded a Philippine island where American soldiers were stationed. After a military scuffle, the Japanese won the battle and took control of the island, putting the captured Americans in a prison camp.

This particular island was very remote, and direct communication with the Japanese army high command rarely took place. One day a plane flew over the island dropping leaflets. When the Japanese soldiers picked up the leaflets and read them, they learned for the first time that World War II had ended—and they had lost!

As I understand it, the Japanese soldiers brought the news to their colonel, who promptly opened all the jail doors and let the prisoners out. Then the colonel walked over to the American commander and said, "We are now your prisoners. You have won the war."

One minute the American soldiers were prisoners, and the next they were set free. Essentially, they were free even while still held captive, but they were kept captive through lack of knowledge that the war had ended. But when knowledge hit that island, they were freed!

Similarly, you've already been freed. And I believe God is saying to you, "It's time for you to break out of *your* captivity of poverty and lack." How do you do it? Through knowing the Word.

The answer to every problem you might go through is in the Word, but you have to break out of the arena of ignorance. You must know what the Bible says to receive revelation of God's truth and apply His principles of increase to your life. Then you actually activate His power to set you free from poverty, lack, and any other yoke of the enemy.

The Key to a Life of Blessing And Prosperity is Knowledge

The New Testament says something else about the consequences of not knowing God's Word:

> **Their** [the Gentiles'] **moral understanding is darkened and their reasoning is beclouded. [They are] alienated (estranged, self-banished) from the life of God—with no share in it. [This is] because of the ignorance—the want of knowledge and perception, the willful blindness—that is deep-seated in them, due to their hardness of heart (to the insensitiveness of their moral nature).**
> —Ephesians 4:18

This verse says that unbelievers are alienated from, or non-participants of, the life God wants for them.

What is the key to God's abundant life? Knowledge. And what causes alienation from an abundant life of blessings and prosperity? Ignorance.

The enemy's strategy is obvious. He knows that only knowledge of God's principles found in the Word can bring you into the prosperity God intends for you to enjoy, so to keep you from participating in the life of God, he uses every means he can to keep you ignorant of the Word.

God Gives Wisdom and Knowledge

The devil may be in the business of keeping you ignorant of God's Word, but I have good news for you: God is in the business of delivering you *out* of ignorance! Indeed, God is the Giver of wisdom and knowledge:

> **For to the person who pleases Him God gives WISDOM and KNOWLEDGE and joy; but to the sinner He gives the work of gathering and heaping up, that he may give to one who pleases God.**
>
> —Ecclesiastes 2:26

According to this verse, if we desire God's wisdom and knowledge, we must first please Him. The only way to please God is *by faith* (Hebrews 11:6). We walk by faith, talk by faith—do *everything* by faith in order to please God.

To those who please God with their lifestyle of faith, He gives wisdom. *Wisdom* simply means God's common sense, the correct application of His Word.

You see, wisdom must accompany knowledge in order for the latter to be effective. Consequently, quoting the Word in itself doesn't count for a hill of beans; even the devil can quote the Word, which is why reading Scriptures in context is so important. Only as we correctly apply God's Word by His wisdom does the Word transform our lives.

While it's true that God is in the wisdom and knowledge-giving business, too many times we seek God for what we want rather than for what He gives, which is knowledge of His Word and the wisdom to apply it. In other words, we ask Him to make us a success rather than seeking His wisdom in order to succeed.

You know, businessmen come to me and say, "Nasir, I have no time to study the Bible or pray the way I should. I'm working night and day to get my business off the ground. You don't know what it's like to build a business—I have to put in twelve to fifteen hours a day!"

But I do know what it's like to build a business. During a twenty-five year span, I started and owned several businesses, and in that time I learned this: I'm limited in my wisdom and ability, but I serve One who is unlimited.

I serve One who knows finances and business better than I do and who brings me orders, customers, witty ideas, and divine appointments.

Those businessmen don't understand that, so they fulfill the wrong role. They're busy gathering and heaping up, but according to Ecclesiastes 2:26, that's the sinner's job!

In fact, many Christians in business make decisions and then run to God, asking Him to bless the decisions they've already made. But God says, "Are you kidding Me? How can I bless that? If you had come to Me before you made a decision, your plan would already be blessed; you wouldn't need to pray about it now."

Christian businessmen should first be seeking God for His wisdom and knowledge.

"No, I don't have time to seek God. I'm busy working," someone might protest. But that's the problem—too much gathering and heaping up and not enough seeking!

You see, it's never an issue of time; it's an issue of *priorities*.

As I mentioned, God gives the work of gathering and heaping up to the sinner so He can in turn transfer that wealth to those who believe and trust Him. Notice that God doesn't transfer the sinner's wealth to every believer, but only to *those who please Him*.

That transfer of wealth can happen in many ways. Maybe you can only think of a few ways for God to get finances to you, but God can think of a million! That's why it's integral for you to seek His wisdom in all your business dealings.

God's Knowledge and Ideas Lead to Prosperity

So let Jesus be your Chief Executive Officer and the Spirit of God your Senior Partner. The Holy Spirit promises to help you make decisions, guiding and directing you in line with His own ways.

As you spend time in the Word and trust in God's wisdom, He actually helps you build your business. And God not only gives you knowledge of His Word, He also gives you knowledge in the natural realm, inspiring ideas that lead you into prosperity.

For example, I know a man named Leroy Anderson who was a pastor for twenty years when God told him to resign his pastorate.

At first Leroy sat around groping for ideas of what to do with his time. One day God spoke to his spirit, saying, "I called you out of the pulpit, not out of the ministry. Now I'm calling you to the ministry of giving."

"How am I going to fulfill that ministry?" Leroy asked.

"I'm going to give you an idea," the Lord answered.

It wasn't long before Leroy got an idea straight from heaven, although to some it seemed silly. God gave him the idea to design a yo-yo with a light bulb inside it.

A yo-yo with lights—that simple idea made that man a fortune. Today he is called "The Yo-Yo King." He owns the largest yo-yo company in North America, and he invests 50 percent of his profits into the Gospel.

God didn't just give this man money; He gave him knowledge. God is in the knowledge-giving business.

Today we are seeing the greatest outpouring of knowledge this world has ever seen. For example, look at the computer industry. Manufacturers can't make computers fast enough. By the time they release the latest computer on the market, it's already outdated.

God is the Source of this outpouring of knowledge, and He endeavors to give knowledge and ideas first to Christians all over this planet. But a great many Christians are sitting on those good ideas, doing nothing with them. They may go around telling people about their God-given idea, but while they're still talking, someone else goes out and invents it!

You see, just because God gives you an idea doesn't mean anything will ever come of it. You'll have to do something with that idea to bring it to pass.

A man once told me, "Nasir, you know those digital cameras for sale now—the kind that you plug into the computer in order to take photos? God gave me that idea three years before the invention showed up on the market."

I asked, "What did you do with the idea?"

"Nothing," he said. "And when I saw digital cameras come out on the market, I got on my knees and repented before the Lord. I said, 'God, You gave me that idea and told me how to put it together three years ago, and I didn't move on it. Father, forgive me. I promise You, if You will trust me with another idea, I'll move on it.'"

So when God gives you an idea, step out in faith and follow through on it. Don't just leave it on the shelf— check it out, do some research, and proceed with it.

You may say, "Yes, but I can't do what it's going to take to make that idea a reality."

You're right, *you* can't do it — but God can! Success is within your grasp in *any* area of your life when you act on the wisdom and knowledge He gives! Remember, Satan's greatest weapon against you is to keep you out of God's Word. But as you break that barrier and feed on the Word, God promises to give you knowledge and wisdom—your keys to prosperity!

Chapter 5
Our Part in Receiving Prosperity—Do the Word

> "Only be strong and very courageous, that you
> may observe to do according to all the law which
> Moses My servant commanded you; do not turn
> from it to the right hand or to the left, that you
> may prosper wherever you go."
>
> —Joshua 1:7 NKJV

Two realms make up this world: the natural and the spiritual. We access the natural realm through the body with its five physical senses. But the spiritual realm, which we can't access through the senses, is more real than the natural realm. In fact, God, whom you can't see with your natural eyes, created the things you do see.

Within the spiritual realm dwells a very real enemy, the devil, who tries to steal, kill, and destroy everything good in our lives (John 10:10). If we choose to live only in the natural realm, we won't even perceive the enemy's strategies against us and we'll be defeated by his every attack.

But I believe God is saying, "If you will cross over the bridge from the natural to the spiritual realm, you will defeat the enemy every single time." What is that bridge? The Word of God!

Now apply that truth to your future prosperity. Your part in crossing the bridge from chronic lack, the natural realm, to supernatural prosperity, the spiritual realm, is found in three simple words: *do the Word.* What I mean by that is, find Scriptures which promise you prosperity, and stand on them in faith!

But realize that the moment you decide to stand on God's Word for prosperity, the enemy will try to attack your finances. Remember, he wants to uproot the Word you've planted in your heart.

You see, the devil most fears the Spirit-filled believer who knows his rights in Christ and who marches forward, acting on the Word. Even the gates of hell can't stand against the child of God who uses the sword of God's Word in faith—in other words, a believer who is a doer of the Word.

God's Command to Joshua

God's purpose in exhorting Joshua to **"do according to all the law"** (Joshua 1:7 NKJV) was to show him the part he played in receiving his prosperity—to do the Word.

At this point in Joshua's life, God had just promoted him as the leader of Israel, a nation of more than three million people. Joshua's subsequent responsibilities included leading the Israelites into the Promised Land—a major undertaking, to say the least.

Now God had already given the Israelites the land, but for forty years they had roamed the desert, surviving in the land of Barely Enough when they could have been living in a land flowing with milk and honey (Numbers 14:8).

God hadn't wanted the Israelites to wander in the wilderness for so many years, only to die in the desert without ever entering the Promised Land. But some of the people brought that sad end upon themselves. Instead of mixing faith with God's promise of entering the land, they believed the ten spies' evil report: "There are giants in the land, and we are grasshoppers in their sight!" (Numbers 13:32,33).

So in Joshua chapter 1, God endeavors a second time to help the Israelites enter and possess the Promised Land. To equip Joshua for the task of leading the Israelites, God instructs him in universal laws that govern both the natural and the spiritual realms.

First, God says, **"No man shall be able to stand before you all the days of your life; as I was with Moses, so I will be with you. I will not leave you nor forsake you"** (v. 5 NKJV).

That's quite a promise to give Joshua! Think of all Moses achieved in his life because God was with him. Now God promises to abide with Joshua in the same way, never leaving nor forsaking him.

Where have we heard that promise before? It's the same promise God gives *us* in Hebrews 13:5!

That means the God who was with Moses and Joshua, making them successful, is the same God who lives inside you and me! We have the same right to say, "God will never leave or forsake *me*. Because He's with me all the time, no enemy can defeat me. Nothing can stop me from possessing my promised land, which includes financial success!"

Once you grasp the fact that the One with Joshua and Moses dwells within you to prosper you wherever you go, you won't make excuses for financial failure anymore. You will no longer think, "Maybe I'm broke because of my upbringing or my education. Maybe I was just born on the wrong side of the tracks."

So Joshua, equipped with the promise of God's help, wonders, "What's my part in possessing the land? Is it to plan the battle strategy? Is it to lead the battle?"

God's answer is, in effect, "Joshua, your only part as leader is to do the Word. And if you obey, you will successfully lead the entire nation of Israel into the land of their inheritance."

God's message to Joshua remains His message to us today: "Prosperity is in your hands. You control it, and your part is to do My Word."

Being a doer of the Word is vital to your success! Jesus is not interested in how many Scriptures you know; He's interested in how many Scriptures you *do*. The only Word that activates God's power to change your situation is the Word you do.

What Joshua did with the Word determined his own success as well as the success of an entire nation. So much rode on Joshua's obedience to do his part.

Verse 7 also says Joshua's part was not only to do the Word but to do according to *all* the law. In other words, God didn't tell him to choose the Scriptures he liked and ignore the rest.

The same goes for us. We can't just pick the Scriptures we like and apply only those to our lives. Nor should we say, "I like these prayers, but not that passage on giving. I like this Scripture on worshipping, but I don't like the one about presenting my body as a living sacrifice." No, God has commanded us to obey *all* the Word.

Now let's look at the next verse:

This Book of the Law shall not depart from your mouth, but you shall meditate in it day and night, that you may observe to do according to all that is written in it. For then you will make your way prosperous, and then you will have good success.
—Joshua 1:8 NKJV

Notice that it says *you* make your way prosperous. Now if Joshua had the ability to make his way prosperous, then you and I possess that same ability.

You may ask, "Do you mean I've been waiting all this time on the Lord to make my business explode or to pay off my debts, and *I'm* actually the one who brings about my own prosperity?"

That's exactly right. Prosperity has been in our hands all along, but if we won't do the Word, we won't participate in God's abundant life.

"You're telling me that I can guarantee success in my life if I do the Word?" Yes, that's what I'm telling you! "And you're saying the Word always works?" Always.

I know that the Word always works because the Bible says not one word from the mouth of God is devoid of His power (Isaiah 55:11). "And if I stand on the Word, I cannot fail?" Absolutely, because the Word cannot fail. Heaven and earth will pass away before the Word does (Matthew 24:35).

According to God's unfailing Word, we can make our way prosperous! But these verses in Joshua 1 show us that we need also to obey God's admonition to be strong and courageous.

Be Strong and Courageous

The first time I read God's command to Joshua to "be strong and very courageous," I felt sorry for Joshua. God even repeated it to Joshua *four times* in one chapter (vv. 6,7,9,18)!

I thought, *This man had to lead an entire nation into enemy territory, and it sounds like he was a skinny little guy who was afraid of the giants in the land. That must be why God had to remind him to be strong and courageous.*

But the Spirit of God corrected me, "The reason I told Joshua to be strong and courageous," He said, "had nothing to do with his lack of physical strength or courage. Joshua wasn't afraid to go into battle. Remember, Joshua and Caleb were the only two men who returned from spying out the land, exclaiming, 'We can take on those giants and win [Num. 14:9]!'"

So why did God continually encourage Joshua to remain strong? What would he face that would require great strength and courage? Think about what it must have been like for Joshua as the Israelites prepared to enter the Promised Land.

Picture Joshua spending time with God. He prays, "Okay, Lord, I'm ready to take Your people into the Promised Land. Tell me what I have to do." God gives him the plan for the first conquest: the city of Jericho.

Later Joshua calls a meeting with all the generals and captains of the army. They gather around Joshua and ask, "Have you seen the walls? They're so thick, the people of Jericho hold chariot races on them!

"So what's the plan, Joshua? How and when do we attack? What weapons do we use? How do we get through those walls to win this battle?"

Joshua replies, "Well, guys, you better sit down for this news. I prayed, and God told me the plan. This is the word of the Lord to us. We're going to surround the city..."

"Oh, good, Joshua!" they responded. "Are we going to climb the walls? Ram the gates till we break through? Siege the city until they run out of food and water?"

"No, no, no. All of those are good ideas, but here's what we're going to do instead. We're going to march around the city every day for seven days."

"Oh, well, okay. But then on the seventh day we attack, right?"

"No, no, no. We *shout*."

"What? We're going to march around the city and then shout? Joshua, have you had too much sun? What kind of battle strategy is that? The soldiers are just going to laugh at us when we tell them your intentions!"

Can you imagine how ridiculous God's plan must have sounded to the Israelites? Joshua no doubt faced considerable opposition from them, not to mention the scorn and insults of enemy soldiers who watched the mysterious seven-day march from atop the walls.

Think of the pressure that must have weighed on Joshua those seven days. It would have been so easy for him to say, "Let's forget that plan and just attack!"

But God's words rang in Joshua's ears: "Be strong and very courageous." That divine admonition helped him keep standing on the Lord's Word until His plan succeeded and the walls crashed down.

Why did Joshua need courage? He needed it because it's difficult to do the Word when everyone around you is saying it won't work. It takes courage to maintain that stand and refuse to be moved from what the Word says when no one else is standing with you.

Don't Be Distracted From Standing on the Word

You see, when you make a stand not to compromise God's Word, often all hell breaks loose against you. First, the enemy tries to keep you away from hearing the Word. And if that doesn't work, he tries to distract you from the Word you are hearing.

For instance, as you're in church and the pastor preaches the Word, the enemy may send thoughts your way to distract you. You might begin thinking, *How am I going to redesign that brochure at work?* or *I have to remember to add salt to the roast for lunch.* Meanwhile, you're missing half the sermon!

Afterwards you say, "That was a good sermon." But how are you going to apply it to your life when you didn't really listen to it?

Maybe you protest, "I don't know, but I felt good listening to it." But if what you heard doesn't change something about how you think, speak, or act, then you missed what God was trying to get across to you.

"But I can quote the Scripture text the pastor used!" Yes, but if you're not living that Scripture, you don't have the revelation of it yet.

Don't Abandon the Word Because Of Persecution or Temptation

However, once you do receive the revelation of a Scripture, the devil's next strategy is to do everything he possibly can to make you abandon your beliefs. He'll send persecution from the right and temptations from the left— anything to make you compromise or give up on the Word.

We can see in the book of Acts that the enemy sends persecution so believers will abandon the Word. The apostle Paul made three missionary journeys, returning to the three towns—Lystra, Derby, and Iconium—where people had persecuted him, caused riots, and even stoned him and left him for dead. (Acts 14:1-22.)

Why did Paul return to those towns? He risked his life in order to strengthen the towns' new converts spiritually so they wouldn't abandon their belief in God's Word during times of persecution.

I've noticed that the more you stand on the Word, the more persecution is likely to come against you. The moment you make a decision to pursue God's principles of financial increase, Satan will try to steal that Word from you.

That's why God said to Joshua, in effect, "You can be strong and courageous because I've given you My Word. What My Word says is so contrary to the way the world thinks that people may laugh at you and some may even think you're crazy. But that's why you'll have to stand strong and be courageous."

The same holds true for you. You need strength and courage, not just in the area of finances, but in *every* area of life, because when Satan attacks you from the right and the left, you'd better know beyond a shadow of a doubt that you're not moving from your stand on God's Word.

You see, you can learn God's principles of financial increase, but those principles won't do you any good if you give up on them as soon as you encounter times of trouble or persecution.

And those times *will* come. Unexpected bills may show up. The car may break down. You may have a flat tire. But those circumstances are all part of the enemy's attempt to keep you from standing on the Word. Determine that you won't let him succeed!

The truth is, the enemy doesn't have any new tricks. He's still using the old flat-tire trick or the broken-down-car trick. He doesn't care if his tricks are old, as long as they still work.

But you can make sure that the devil's strategies *don't* work in your life anymore. How? By making the decision that you will stand firm on the Word no matter what pressure or opposition you face. You must be strong and very courageous in order to prosper wherever you go.

And wherever means *everywhere*—in the city or in the country, at home or at your job. Wherever you go, whatever you put your hand to, prosperity will follow you if you do the Word.

So keep the Word before you. Read it. Hear it. Get it into your heart. Speak it with your mouth. Meditate on it day and night.

By doing so you make God's promises more real in your heart than the natural circumstances around you and you cross over the bridge from the natural to the spiritual realm—from chronic lack to supernatural prosperity. Meditating on the Word enables you to do all that is written in God's Word.

God's Covenant—A Conditional Promise

When it comes down to it, it is our obligation to do the Word if we want to receive prosperity.

Nowhere is the truth that we hold our future prosperity in our own hands more clearly set forth than in Deuteronomy 28, where God contrasts the blessings of the covenant with the curse of the law.

Before God lists all the blessings His people can experience as part of the covenant, He starts verse 1 with a big "if." Whenever I see an *if* in the Word, I apply the brakes and stop to check it out. The word *if* usually flags a condition following—the man-ward part of a divine promise. Let's see what this particular *if* refers to:

IF you will listen diligently to the voice of the Lord your God, being watchful to do all His commandments which I command you this day, the Lord your God will set you high above all the nations of the earth,
And all these blessings shall come upon you and overtake you, IF you heed the voice of the Lord your God.

—Deuteronomy 28:1,2

God tells us there are two ifs or conditions we must fulfill. First, we must listen to the voice of the Lord. No matter what He tells us to do, we are to obey without even stopping to think about it.

Second, we must do what is written in God's Word. Notice that after we fulfill our part of the condition, the Bible says all of God's blessings shall come upon us and overtake us.

What blessings is God talking about here? Deuteronomy 28 goes on to say that you'll be blessed in the city, blessed in the field, blessed in your family, blessed coming in, and blessed going out. In other words, you'll be blessed in every area of your life!

Verses 4 and 5 continue, promising that you'll be blessed in your ground, blessed in your cattle, and blessed in your basket. The blessed ground and basket refer to the rich, fertile soil which produces an abundant harvest. Blessed cattle are those that are healthy and multiply exceedingly.

In today's terms, that translates as blessings in your job or business, getting raises and promotions or new customers and orders.

Verse 8 goes on to say that the Lord will command blessings upon your storehouse, or the place you store your substance. Today that might refer to your bank account.

God has a lot of blessings to pour out on you. If you want those blessings to come upon you and overtake you, make sure you fulfill the conditions in verse 1: Listen to the voice of the Lord, and do His Word.

God's Blessings Will *Overtake* You

I find it significant that God said, "All of these blessings will *overtake* you." Think about it. You can't be overtaken by something that's in front of you. When you're driving down the road, only the cars behind you can overtake you. Therefore, if God's blessings can overtake you, they must be behind you as well!

When I finally understood that principle, it changed my life. I realized for the first time that if God's blessings are behind me, my eyes should definitely *not* be on the blessings, or I'd be looking backwards.

That's the problem with too many believers. Their eyes are on the blessings, yet they don't understand why they are not seeing them manifested in their lives. "Where is my blessing, Lord? I've been looking for it," they say.

That attitude spells trouble. As long as Christians are looking for their blessing, their blessing won't look for them!

I once asked the Lord, "If our eyes are not to be on the blessings, what *should* we focus on?"

The Lord responded, "All blessings originate in Me. If you keep your eyes on Me, the blessings will overtake you."

All of God's blessings move full speed toward Him—the same direction we move if we're focused on God. But the blessings move faster than we do.

Now that I understand this truth, my eyes are not on the blessings; they're on Jesus. His will is my will. My focus is now, what does *He* want? What is *His* purpose for my life?

I focus on Him by feeding on His Word and listening for His voice. Therefore, I don't have to be concerned about looking for blessings. They are all looking for me as I concentrate on doing God's Word.

Stop chasing your blessings, because you will never catch them. But you *can* let them chase *you* by focusing on and doing the Word of God. And those blessings will eventually overtake you. You don't have to worry or even think about them; they will hunt you down, and you will experience blessing upon blessing upon blessing in every area of your life.

The bottom line is this: The prosperity message is not, *Keep your eyes on prosperity.* Biblical prosperity comes *as we keep our eyes on God.*

Redeemed From the Curse of the Law

In Deuteronomy 28, after God finishes talking about the blessings of obedience, He lists all the curses that result from *not* doing God's Word (vv. 28:15-68).

I'm not going to dwell on those curses, but I want you to understand this: If you are still living under any part of the curse of the law, it isn't Jesus' responsibility; it's *yours*—your responsibility to fulfill the conditions of hearkening to God's voice and obeying all of His Word.

Jesus already redeemed you from the curse of the law. He paid for your freedom with His own blood.

Christ purchased our freedom (redeeming us) from the curse (doom) of the Law's (condemnation), by [Himself] becoming a curse for us, for it is written [in the Scriptures], Cursed is everyone who hangs on a tree (is crucified).

—Galatians 3:13

Part of the curse of the law is poverty. But Jesus redeemed us from poverty—we don't have to be poor anymore! Nonetheless, we can still choose to live in lack by not following God's principles of increase. And if we do, that's our fault, not God's.

Now if we're not under the curse, then where are we? We are not only redeemed *from* something, we are also redeemed *to* something:

To the end that through [their receiving] Christ Jesus, the blessing [promised] to Abraham might come upon the Gentiles, so that we through faith might [all] receive [the realization of] the promise of the (Holy) Spirit.

—v. 14

The Bible goes on to say that we are Abraham's offspring and heirs according to the promise (Galatians 3:29). Jesus redeemed us from the curse of the law so we can inherit the promise God gave to Abraham.

We've already seen that God's covenant with Abraham included three promises. He told Abraham that 1) He would make him the father of many nations (Genesis 17:4); 2) He would richly bless him (Genesis 12:2); and 3) He would make Abraham a blessing to others (Genesis 12:2).

God told Abraham to take his wife Sarah and all of their possessions and leave his homeland. Abraham didn't even know where he was going, but he trusted God and went anyway.

Abraham didn't possess much when he left the land of Ur. But God kept His Word and blessed him: **"And Abram was very rich in cattle, in silver, and in gold"** (Genesis 13:2 KJV).

God richly blessed Abraham financially and materially— and as his heirs, we're next in line! As we've seen, our part in receiving the blessings of God's covenant with Abraham is to hearken unto *God's* voice and obey all of His Word.

Fulfilling those divine conditions not only keeps us free from the curse of the law, but it enables God to bless us abundantly with the blessings of Abraham. That in turn enables us to be the blessing God intends us to be in this world!

Establish the Image of the Word In Your Spirit

So to experience the blessings of Abraham, we must be doers of the Word. James compares the person who hears the Word and doesn't do it to **"...a man who looks carefully at his [own] natural face in a mirror; For he thoughtfully observes himself, then goes off and promptly forgets what he was like"** (James 1:23,24).

You see, the Word acts as a spiritual mirror. When we read the Bible, its words of truth form an image on the inside of us.

Here's an example. Suppose you read the verse in which Jesus says, **"I am come that they might have life, and that they might have it more abundantly"** (John 10:10 KJV).

Now what do you see when you meditate on those words? Do you see yourself broke, barely able to pay your bills? No, you should see yourself living an abundant life—that's the image the Word should form in your heart.

The problem is, after that image forms in your heart, you still have to *do* the Word before it will change your life. In other words, apply the Word in your thoughts, words, and actions.

But too many times we make the mistake described in James 1:24. We fail to apply the Word we heard; therefore, we soon forget the image we saw in God's mirror—His Word.

How do we bring back that image once it has faded from our hearts through neglect? The key can be found in the following verse: **"Let them SAY CONTINUALLY, 'Let the Lord be magnified, who has pleasure in the prosperity of His servant'"** (Psalm 35:27 NKJV).

As we begin to do the Word by continually speaking words of faith, the image of God's taking pleasure in the prosperity of His servants will become established in our hearts. Eventually it will become so much a part of us that we'll never again forget to see ourselves prosperous according to the image of His Word.

The more you speak the Word, the clearer the image of prosperity becomes on the inside of you. That's the Word-based image you want to focus on. Refuse to forget or abandon it, for when you hold fast to that image, you begin to live God's abundant life.

Stand strong on God's Word—no matter what attacks or distractions the devil brings against you. By doing the Word you can cross over the bridge from the natural realm into the spiritual realm of supernatural prosperity!

Chapter 6
The Condition to Prosperity—
Seek God's Higher Ways

"**And he** [King Uzziah] **sought God in the days of Zechariah...and AS LONG AS HE SOUGHT THE LORD, GOD MADE HIM TO PROSPER.**"
—2 Chronicles 26:5 KJV

God's will is that we prosper in life, but that doesn't mean prosperity will automatically happen. Remember, there is a man-ward and a God-ward function to every promise. Second Chronicles 26:5 tells us that the man-ward function or condition to prosperity is to seek God's higher ways.

You see, as long as King Uzziah sought the Lord—as long as he was hungry for the Word and did what God wanted him to do—God made him prosper.

The same is true for us. As long as we seek God and His Word, you and I will experience prosperity in our lives.

Too often, Christians want to prosper without doing their part by seeking God. But it doesn't work that way. The Bible says we must seek first God's kingdom (Matthew 6:33). Only then will His blessings be added unto us.

Let's look at that verse in context, starting at verse 24. Jesus starts out this passage of Scripture by saying we cannot serve both God and mammon—money: **"No one can serve two masters; for either he will hate the one and love the other, or he will stand by and be devoted to the one and despise and be against the other. You cannot serve God and mammon [that is, deceitful riches, money, possessions or what is trusted in]."**

Actually, Jesus' message in this passage is that you cannot put your trust in both money and God. If money serves as the source of your security, then you're not putting your faith in God as your Source.

Jesus goes on to say:

Therefore I tell you, stop being perpetually uneasy (anxious and worried) about your life, what you shall eat or what you shall drink, and about your body, what you shall put on. Is not life greater [in quality] than food, and the body [far above and more excellent] than clothing?
...And which of you by worrying and being anxious can add one unit of measure [cubit] to his stature or to the span of his life?

—vv. 25,27

In essence, Jesus said, "Stop worrying about daily life necessities!"

If you're worried and concerned about what you should eat, drink, or wear, you might as well put your trust in mammon!

Jesus puts it something like this, "If your Heavenly Father keeps feeding the birds, why do you think *you* have to trust in mammon? Don't you think you're worth more to Him than birds?" (v. 26).

Certainly, the God who takes care of birds can find a way to take care of you. And He has the ability, the resources, and the desire to do it.

So stop worrying. No matter what financial struggle you're facing, rest assured that God will bring you through it and meet your need.

"But I don't know how I'm going to pay my rent!" you say. Take a deep breath and relax. Remember, God operates through faith.

You see, the root of worry is fear. If you're worried about something, you're in fear, not faith, about that particular matter, which hinders God from moving on your behalf. Worry also shortens your life and consumes precious time that you could use to seek God.

Jesus communicates to us in these verses. We do not need to worry about getting our basic needs met. God will take care of us in the area of finances as long as we're seeking Him and walking in obedience to His Word.

Despite Jesus' admonition not to worry, the majority of Christians still do! God's higher ways haven't become revelation in their hearts.

You may say, "Yes, but you don't understand the financial problems I'm struggling against in my life right now." Hasn't God delivered you from difficult times in your life in the past? The same God can bring you through today and into tomorrow victoriously!

Once you get ahold of this truth, you'll stop worrying about all of your tomorrows. You will no longer expect mammon to take care of your future instead of God. Why? You no longer need worry because the God who originally created tomorrow is the One who delivered you out of yesterday's trials to bring you triumphantly to today!

We're often so concerned about how we're going to take care of tomorrow's bills or financial worries. Why don't we just trust our Heavenly Father to take care of us?

> **Therefore do not worry and be anxious, saying, What are we going to have to eat? or, What are we going to have to drink? or, What are we going to have to wear?**
> **For the Gentiles (heathen) wish for and crave and diligently seek after all these things; and your heavenly Father well knows that you need them all.**
> —Matthew 6:31,32

You can not worry and be in faith, nor can you put yourself and God first simultaneously. When you focus all your attention on taking care of your own needs—such as what you'll eat, where you'll live, or what you'll wear—you have just put yourself first. That's what the world does, but as a child of God, you're supposed to be different; you're to put God first and then watch Him take care of your needs.

We either know God or we don't. He is either a Provider or He isn't. But if we know Him, we get a revelation of His character as our Provider.

Jesus is essentially telling us in these verses, "Get a revelation of the character of your loving Heavenly Father! If you don't know Him, how can you ever trust Him? Know that the Father feeds the birds of the air and clothes the lilies of the field, yet He loves you so much more than these!"

Seek God and His Ways

Once you get a revelation of your Father's character, no circumstances need ever hold you back again. You won't worry about getting your needs met. You won't spend all your time serving mammon or seeking after meeting your material needs. Instead, you'll rest in the assurance of your Heavenly Father's love as you obey Jesus' admonition:

But SEEK YE FIRST THE KINGDOM OF GOD, and his righteousness; and all these things shall be added unto you.

—Matthew 6:33 KJV

Notice that this verse starts with the word *but*. That word is there for a reason because the Bible contains no meaningless words. Let's look at the context to figure out why.

Jesus has just finished talking about what non-believers do—they put themselves and their needs first. Now He's saying, "But don't do as the world does, seeking after daily necessities and material things as your main focus. Seek first My kingdom and My ways, and cast those cares on Me."

You see, if you do what the world does, you will get the results the world gets. But for things to change in your life, *you* have to change! We know that God doesn't change, and His Word doesn't change; so that means if you have been suffering lack and you want to become prosperous, you are the one who will have to do something different.

We often keep doing things the same way we've always done them, making the same mistakes that have kept us in lack in the past. Then out of frustration we ask, "Why am I not becoming prosperous, Lord?" But we won't see prosperity until we change our ways, becoming serious about seeking God first.

To seek God means to hunt, search for, and diligently pursue the knowledge of His ways, digging into the Bible every day. That's the only way you'll discover more of the kingdom principles and mysteries of God.

The Lord once gave me an illustration to help me understand what He means by seeking Him.

Imagine that you're running late for an important appointment and you can't find your car keys. What do you do? You don't just casually glance around and then give up if

81

you can't locate your keys right away. No, you begin to earnestly *seek* them!

You turn the living room upside down, hunting for those keys. You turn the bedroom and kitchen upside down. You look in every nook and cranny, and you don't stop seeking until you find them.

That same kind of intensity and hunger should consume you as you seek to know God and His ways. Channel all the extra time you used to spend worrying into hungering and thirsting after His Word!

Seek God *First*

I probably read Matthew 6:33 hundreds of times before the word *"first"* jumped out at me. Seek first God's kingdom. Where do you find out about His kingdom? Again, in His Word.

I was reading this verse one day, and on the inside of me the Spirit of God asked, "What does *first* mean?"

"Well, Lord, that's obvious. First means first!"

"That's right," the Lord said. "So what if you get out of bed in the morning, take a shower, put on your clothes, make a cup of coffee, and *then* read your Bible? What's wrong with that? Nothing, except that you've just put My Word fourth, not first, in your day."

The days of playing Christianity are over, friend. We either seek God first or we don't. And it doesn't matter how you look at *first*—it doesn't mean *second*. It doesn't mean *third, fourth,* or *at the end of the day* either.

Here's a sample of the reasoning process we often go through regarding spending time with God. See if it sounds familiar.

If I take a shower when I first wake up, then I'll be more awake to read my Bible. And, of course, if I take a shower I'll have to put my clothes on. But if I go ahead and eat breakfast and drink a cup of coffee, then I'll be even more awake and I'll really be able to get into the Word.

But sometimes I run late, and I don't get a chance to read my Bible after breakfast. So I take it with me, figuring I'll read it once I get to the office.

The problem is, when I arrive at the office, there is a pile of phone messages. I think, *Oh, I better call so-and-so and take care of that situation. I'll read my Bible later on this morning.* But it doesn't quite happen, so I decide to read it during lunchtime.

Then someone calls, and I use my lunch break talking to him. So I decide to read the Bible sometime during the afternoon. But the day slips by so quickly, I never get around to it. Finally, I decide I'll read it when I get home.

When I arrive home, I'm so hungry that I think, *If I don't eat supper, I won't be able to concentrate on my Bible.* Then after I eat, I feel like relaxing for a while, so I turn on the television. I decide to read my Bible when I go to bed, when the house is quiet and peaceful and no one is distracting me.

I climb into bed and pick up my Bible, but before I've read one paragraph, my eyes start to droop. I hadn't realized how tired I was. I yawn and think, *I'll just read the Bible in the morning when I'm fresh.*

I set the alarm to get up a little earlier than normal. But the next morning when the alarm clock rings, I press the snooze button.

(I'm convinced that the snooze button came from the pit of hell, because it has kept so many Christians from seeking God first in their day! Their flesh says, "I'll do it tomorrow. I have to sleep a little more today." But there is no record of anyone ever dying because they got up earlier every morning to seek God first!)

So as a result of all that carnal reasoning, first becomes last. The days go by, and my Bible gets very little use as I seek *last* the kingdom of God—*if* I can squeeze time for the Word into my day at all!

Too often that's the way we go through life. We don't give God our best by seeking Him first, but instead we give Him a tiny bit of our worst. We wait to open our Bible (if we do it at all!) until we're exhausted, drained of energy, and want nothing more than to sleep. Then we wonder why we're not blessed!

God wants to take you up higher than you've ever gone before in your spiritual walk, but you won't get there without some serious discipline.

As I said earlier, it's never an issue of time—no one has more than twenty-four hours in a day—but it is an issue of priority.

You will not seek God first until you make it a priority. Once you realize that spending time with God is more important than anything else you could possibly do in a day, you will do whatever is necessary to make sure you seek Him first. And I promise you that as you give Him the highest priority every day, your life will change.

That's what happened with me. My life began to change drastically the day I made the decision to start spending time with God as soon as I wake up every day. My commitment has grown to the point that now I refuse to do anything until I have first spent my time with God.

The Lord once said very clearly to me, "Nasir, the key to your success is not what you do on Sunday morning; *you find success in your daily routine.* So if you'll give Me the first part of each day, I'll direct the rest of it."

Now every morning when I get out of bed, I seek God first. It was tough at the beginning—my flesh was screaming! But I started with five minutes and grew from there.

But don't legalize what I'm saying here. I *don't* mean you have to get up at three o'clock in the morning to find time to read your Bible before anything else. I'm saying that you need to make it a daily priority to pray and seek God in His Word. If you find that you can do that better in the afternoon, fine—but then discipline yourself to do it!

You Do the Seeking— Let God Do the Adding

So as we seek first God's kingdom principles, or His way of doing things, then God will add to us all the natural things we need in order to live an abundant life. Notice that Matthew 6:33 doesn't say these things *might* be added to us if God is in a good mood. It says they *will* be added to us.

Our job is to do the seeking; God's job is to do the adding. But the adding doesn't come until after we make a conscious decision to seek God's ways.

Too many times *we* try to do the adding and therefore have no time to do the seeking. We fulfill the wrong role!

"But you don't understand, Nasir," you might say. "My neighbor bought a new car, and I've decided we need one too. Besides, my wife has been bugging me to buy a new car, so I'm just going to take the plunge!"

So you go into debt up to your neck in order to "keep up with the Joneses"! That's an example of your doing the adding instead of allowing God to do the adding His way.

Here's another example. A couple I know found out they had inherited several thousand dollars. At the time, this couple was renting an apartment. As they talked over how to use the inheritance money, they totally convinced themselves that they should use it as a down payment on a home worth four times the amount of the inheritance.

There was just one problem with the couple's plan. Even if both of them worked and earned as much overtime pay as possible, they would end up deeply in debt, having barely enough money to make the mortgage payments.

I told the couple, "Don't you understand what the enemy is doing? He's trying to convince you to do the adding instead of allowing God to do it. But if *you* do it, you'll have a yoke around your neck for thirty years!

"Why don't you just buy a less expensive house? Buy one that costs only $20,000 more than the inheritance, and use the inheritance money as a down payment. Then work as hard as you can to pay off the balance, which is a more manageable goal.

"That way you won't be a servant to the lender. You'll only be a servant of God!"

The enemy had this couple so convinced that they had to do the adding in their lives that they thought God was leading them to buy that more expensive house. But they were completely relieved to remember that their part was only to seek God and let *Him* do the adding.

You see, God wouldn't lead His children into a situation where they could barely pay their tithes, much less give offerings, because they're working day and night just to cover their mortgage payment! The Bible says, **"The blessing of the Lord makes one rich, and He adds no sorrow with it"** (Proverbs 10:22 NKJV).

Too often Christians spend their time trying to jump ahead to the fulfillment of their dream for prosperity right away instead of moving toward that dream, knowing it may come gradually. In other words, they're busy adding instead of seeking.

For example, perhaps a friend tells you, "Look at how the Lord has blessed me—I've got a new car!" But you know he's already deeply in debt and having a difficult time making his present payments.

The last thing that person needs to do is take on the additional debt of a new car. Nevertheless, he's out to convince the world that God is the One who blessed him.

But because the friend is busy adding when he should be seeking, the car eventually becomes a curse to him. The thought constantly weighs on his mind, *Somehow I've got to make the car payment this month!*

Now if God tells you to buy a new car, then do it. But don't just buy one because your neighbor did or because you want somehow to prove that God is blessing you. Don't *you* do the adding; let *God* do it.

Hebrews 11:6 gives us the same message. It says, **"He that cometh to God must believe that he is, and that he is a rewarder of them that diligently seek him"** (KJV). You see, we do the seeking; God does the rewarding—and the rewarding comes *after* the seeking.

We Can Know God's Ways

We know what seeking means, we know that we are to seek God first, and that we expect His reward after seeking Him. But *why* are we to seek first God's kingdom and His ways? The Word tells us God's ways are better and higher than our ways.

For my thoughts are not your thoughts, neither are your ways my ways, saith the Lord. For as the heavens are higher than the earth, so are my ways higher than your ways, and my thoughts than your thoughts.

—Isaiah 55:8,9 KJV

These verses tell us God's thoughts don't line up with our thoughts, that His ways differ from our ways. Our human ways are based on the information we perceive from the natural realm by our senses, but God's ways are based on His Word. Therefore, to line up our ways with God's ways, we must govern what we say, think, and do based on the Word of God.

When God said, "My thoughts are not your thoughts," He *wasn't* saying, "I refuse to tell you My thoughts."

Some people think that's what God means. They say, "Oh, you can't know what God's thoughts are—they're too high, and His ways are too mysterious." But that's simply not true. All you have to do is dig into the Bible, and you'll find out God's thoughts and ways. And that is the very reason we do seek Him.

We can know God's thoughts! For example, Jeremiah 29:11 tells us something of God's thoughts: His mind is on us! This verse also gives us some idea of God's thoughts toward us:

For I know the thoughts that I think toward you, saith the Lord, thoughts of peace, and not of evil, to give you an expected end.
—Jeremiah 29:11 KJV

The *New International Version* describes God's thoughts toward you as **"...plans to prosper you and not to harm you, plans to give you hope and a future."**

So we have just discovered one of God's thoughts toward us: He wants to prosper us!

We also know that God thinks the whole world should be saved (2 Peter 3:9). And there are countless other Scriptures which reveal God's thoughts toward us. So you see, although we may not know all the thoughts of God, we *can* know those revealed in His Word.

The Opposite Kingdom

So if it is possible to know God's thoughts, then what *does* God mean when He says, "My thoughts are not your thoughts; My ways are not your ways"? He means that His thoughts and ways are *better* than our thoughts and ways.

Once as I was preaching on this subject, the Spirit of God spoke up on the inside of me, saying, "You could almost call My kingdom *the opposite kingdom*." I took that to mean that His kingdom stands opposite to our "kingdom"—our natural way of thinking. And His way of doing things usually counters the way we do things.

For example, think about the time King Jehoshaphat and the people of Judah faced imminent attack by three armies (2 Chronicles 20:1-25).

What do you do when three armies come against you? You go into battle and fight! But God said, "Go into battle and sing praises to Me." That's definitely *not* what your natural mind would choose to do!

So the people of Judah went into battle singing praises— and they won!

I can give you many examples of how God's ways are not our ways. The world says, "Get all you can, can all you get, sit on the can, and poison the rest!" But God says, "Give."

In troubled times, our natural mind screams, "Worry, worry, worry!" God says, "Receive peace." We protest, "But there's so much to worry about!" He only replies, "I know, but that isn't My way."

No matter what subject you study in the Word, you'll find that God's ways oppose the way we naturally think. That's why He calls His kingdom the opposite kingdom.

God's Ways Always Work

When God says His ways are higher than ours, He also means that His ways always work. His ways always accomplish what He intends them to accomplish.

Man's ways often fail, but you can count on God's ways to succeed. As surely as the rain and snow fall to the earth, so too God's Word always works.

For as the rain cometh down, and the snow from heaven, and returneth not thither, but watereth the earth, and maketh it bring forth and bud, that it may give seed to the sower, and bread to the eater:
So shall my word be that goeth forth out of my mouth: it shall not return unto me void, but it

shall accomplish that which I please, and it shall prosper in the thing whereto I sent it.
—Isaiah 55:10,11 KJV

By making this comparison, God helps us relate the fact that His ways do not fail to do something in nature that we already understand. I mean, you've never seen rain or snow go up instead of down, have you? And you're not surprised when rain or snow fall from the skies, are you? No, you expect it!

Similarly, God says you can trust His ways to work as surely as you can expect the rain and snow to fall down to earth from the heavens!

Think of that—God's ways are guaranteed to work. And once that revelation gets rooted inside you, nothing can shake your faith in Him!

So it's our choice. We can try to prosper according to our own ways, or we can seek to know God's higher ways, which always work.

It's like trying to fix a piece of equipment when we don't know how it works. We can either spend a lot of time trying to figure it out ourselves, or we can simply read the manual, follow the directions, and finish the job.

We often spend years trying to figure out how to solve our financial problems when what we ought to be doing is *seeking first* the ways of God by simply reading the Bible—the divine Manual covering every aspect of life.

We would save ourselves years of heartache if we'd only seek in God's Word *His* way of delivering us from financial lack. Once we know God's way, the next step is to commit ourselves to stop doing things *our* way and start doing them the only way that works!

Ten Percent *How*—Ninety Percent *Why*

A lot of people have sought to know God's ways and kingdom principles, but they don't live them. One day as I was driving down the road, the Lord explained to me why this is so. He said, "Success in My Word is 10 percent *how* and 90 percent *why*."

I asked, "Lord, what do You mean?"

The Lord replied, "Ten percent is knowing the Word and what it will do for you, but ninety percent is knowing why you should obey it."

Suppose I tell you that the love of God has been shed abroad in our hearts (Romans 5:5) and that Jesus gave us one commandment: to love one another (John 15:12). You now know these truths, but does that mean you will suddenly decide to walk in love? No.

Since faith works through love (Galatians 5:6), unless you walk in love, your faith for prosperity in every area of your life won't work.

Now I've told you *why* you should walk in love, not just what the Word says about it. And because you understand the benefits of doing the Word, God's principles on love suddenly become a priority to you.

That's why 90 percent of success in life is knowing *why* you should do the Word. Many Christians have learned the how, but they haven't grasped a revelation of the why yet. So again and again they go around the same mountain of unforgiveness, anger, worry, and so forth, not realizing how much that mountain hinders them from living an abundant life.

Just reading Scriptures doesn't make much difference in your life. When you understand what the Word will do for you on a practical level, when you learn the *why*, you'll grab ahold of it and truly live.

You'll start to say, "Taking offense or holding a grudge against someone costs too much and shuts down the anointing on my life. I have to forgive, because unless I do, I'll keep myself from receiving by faith all God has for me!"

Knowing why you should obey the Word simply gives you the proper motivation. And then it's not difficult to follow God's direction to seek Him and His ways first—the *why* is that He can then add blessings of prosperity to you.

So get a revelation of what learning and applying God's kingdom principles will do for you. Hunger for the Word more than bread. Go after it with everything in you because it is your lifeline; it is your source of success. As you daily seek God first and give Him and His higher ways your priority, His Word will make you prosperous in all areas of life!

Chapter 7
God's Law of Sowing and Reaping

"And He [Jesus] **replied to them** [the disciples]**, To you it has been given to know the secrets and mysteries of the kingdom of heaven, but to them it has not been given."**

—Matthew 13:11

When you have completely settled in your heart that it is God's will for you to prosper and you know your part and conditions to prosperity, you are ready to discover God's principles of prosperity. Jesus refers to these kingdom principles in Matthew 13:11, calling them "the secrets and mysteries of the kingdom of heaven."

The Mysteries of the Kingdom

When I first read this verse, I thought, *Boy, I wish I could have been there when Jesus was giving out those mysteries! Then I'd know His secret counsels too!*

But the Spirit of God spoke up on the inside of me and said, "I didn't just give those secrets and mysteries to the disciples; I wrote them down in the Bible for everyone."

From that day on, the Lord began to take me on a journey to discover these mysteries or kingdom principles. Sharing with you the results of that journey is what this book is all about.

Let's look back at our text. Jesus goes on to explain what happens to the person who perceives the mysteries of the kingdom and applies them to his life:

> **For whoever has [spiritual knowledge], to him will more be given and HE WILL BE FURNISHED RICHLY, so that HE WILL HAVE ABUNDANCE; but from him who has not, even what he has will be taken away.**
>
> —Matthew 13:12

According to this verse, as you begin to learn the mysteries of the kingdom, you can count on more revelation coming. And when you live by the mysteries you learn, Jesus promises that you will be furnished richly with abundance!

There's that word *abundance* again. The God of too much loves to give us more than enough! But it's important to realize that there is a divine connection between the kingdom principles God gives us in His Word and the abundant life Jesus promised in John 10:10. In other words, you must know the principles to live in abundance.

God's kingdom principles describe the way His kingdom works. Not only are they eternal but also unbiased; they work for anyone who puts them into practice.

But a word of warning: according to Matthew 13:12, if you don't walk in the light of what you learn—if you don't renew your mind, thereby prospering your soul—any financial increase you might gain can be lost. You'll have holes in your pockets, and your prosperity will drain away (Haggai 1:6).

The Key to the Mystery—Sowing

Let's look at a similar passage in Mark 4 to see in context what mysteries Jesus referred to. Jesus says to His disciples:

"To you has been entrusted the mystery of the kingdom of God, [that is, the secret counsels of God which are hidden from the ungodly;] but for those outside [of our circle] everything becomes a parable."

—Mark 4:11

The world could listen to Jesus' parables but never fully understand them. But to His disciples Jesus said, "You're not only supposed to *hear* these parables, you're supposed to *understand* what they mean. Hidden in each one is a kingdom principle, an insight into God's way of doing things. The world can't see these principles, but the mystery has been entrusted to *you*."

Notice Jesus didn't say, "The mystery *will be* entrusted to you at some time in the future." He said, "It *has been* entrusted to you"—past tense. You see, He had already given the disciples the mystery; they just hadn't recognized it.

The disciples were just like us. When we're looking for something we assume is hard to find, we may glance at the object a hundred times without even realizing it's in plain sight!

Jesus had just shared the mystery of the parable of the sower with His disciples (vv. 3-8). In verse 3, Jesus says, **"Give attention to this."** In other words, "What follows is very important, so pay attention!" Then He said, **"Behold, A SOWER WENT OUT TO SOW."**

That's a heavy-duty mystery! Remember, Jesus is teaching us about God's ways, which are higher than our ways. Jesus said, "The sower went out to sow." The mystery is found in the word *sow*. What is God's higher way? *Sow!* If we can get ahold of that one key word, it will change our lives!

Jesus said, **"Seek first My ways, and all these things will be added unto you"** (Matthew 6:33). What is His way? Sowing!

And Jesus said here in our text, "I've given you the secret counsel of God" (Mark 4:11). I can just hear the disciples exclaim, "Secret? Oh, my goodness, did anyone write that one down? Jesus just gave us the answer to the mystery!"

What was the mystery? The sower goes out to sow. As He explained this mystery, I imagine Jesus said something like, "Men, you may have a tough time understanding this, but sowing is the key principle of increase. It's the way God's kingdom works. This is God's higher truth—and it works!"

Now you may say, "I thought the mystery would be much deeper than that. It just can't be contained in a little three-letter word like *sow!*" But God wouldn't make His secrets to abundant life so deep that you and I could never discover and grasp them. That isn't the kind of God we serve. He *wants* us to know His kingdom principles!

Sowing is a law God has put into effect on this planet, and it will work for anyone who will work it. Whether you believe it or not, it will still produce in your life!

You can talk to any farmer in any country around the world, and he will tell you, "If I sow seed into the ground, I expect a harvest." That's why I said earlier that the finances you and I need are not in heaven—they're right here on earth. All we have to do is reap them! But there is *no* way to reap a financial harvest without first sowing seed.

'Don't You Get It?'

Even though Jesus walked the earth as the Son of God, He was a human being with feelings just like you and me. I believe He showed some of that human emotion in the next verse when He said, **"Do you not discern and understand this parable? How then [is it possible for] you to discern and understand all the parables?"** (Mark 4:13).

Jesus had just told His disciples that He had given them the secret counsels of God so they could understand how His kingdom worked and thereby enjoy abundant life. But the disciples' only response must have been an uncomprehending, blank look on their faces.

Jesus recognized that the disciples didn't understand what He said, and so He told them something like, "Don't you get it? I just told you one of God's secret kingdom principles. In fact, I just gave you the key to living an abundant life, and all you can do is look at me with blank faces.

"You're supposed to understand! I know the world doesn't get it, but *you're* supposed to. And if you don't understand this mystery, how are you going to understand all the other parables I tell you?"

Jesus was making the point that the mystery in this parable was pivotal to understanding the other principles He taught. In essence He was also imitating, "If you'll apply the mystery I've just given you, you'll enjoy a life of richness and abundance."

So it was critical that the disciples understand the kingdom principle Jesus set forth in this parable. To make sure they grasped it, He repeated the key to the mystery in verse 14: **"The sower sows...."**

A Lifestyle of Sowing

I had read that verse countless times in the past, but one day it suddenly exploded on the inside of me: **The sower sows!**

Let's camp on that thought for a while. What is a sower? A sower is someone who plants seed as a lifestyle, *not* someone who sows every once in a while or whenever he feels like it.

For instance, if you live in a small town and you see the electrician walk by, you could say, "There goes the electrician!" You don't call him an electrician because he tinkers with electric wiring once a year; you call him that because he practices that profession as a *lifestyle*.

Likewise, you can recognize a teacher because he teaches regularly. He doesn't just talk about things he knows one morning a week for five minutes. No, he leads a lifestyle of teaching.

Likewise, a sower is someone who continually sows seed as a lifestyle, daily looking for ways to sow. Sowing is his number-one priority, and in fact, sowing so consumes him that he doesn't even have time to look for the harvest!

The Spirit of God once asked me, "Nasir, when was the last time someone accused you of being a sower?" Ouch! I had to think about that. People had called me a teacher of the Word, but not too many had accused me of being a daily sower.

How about you? Can anyone "accuse" *you* of being a sower?

Don't call yourself a sower unless sowing is your lifestyle, your daily practice. You're a sower when you get up every morning saying, "Lord, everything I am and everything I own belongs to You. Tell me what You want me to give, and I'll give it today. I don't care if it's the brand-new jacket I bought yesterday—if You tell me to give it to someone, I'll give it, because I'm a sower!"

God looks all over this planet for sowers. He looks for people He can trust with the wealth needed for the end-time harvest. But until you get ahold of this principle of sowing and your lifestyle changes to that of a sower, God cannot trust you as a true steward of His wealth.

Some people are saying, "I'm waiting for my millions." But God is whispering in their hearts (if they would listen!), "You're not a sower yet."

"But I give my tithe and my little offerings!" the same people say. Yes, but God is talking about a *lifestyle* of sowing.

You see, God isn't going to trust you with much if you haven't been faithful with a little. What should you do to be faithful with your finances? Should you lock up all your money in a safety deposit box? No, *sow*.

Live the lifestyle of a sower. Change the way you think. Continually ask God who, where, when, and how much— "Who can I bless today, Lord? What do You want me to sow?"

Do you want to be able to write checks for God's kingdom in the thousands or even millions of dollars? Then you have to prove to God beyond a shadow of a doubt that *today* you are a faithful sower.

So be faithful with what you have now. Prove to God that you will live a lifestyle of sowing. I don't mean just today and tomorrow—I mean from this day forward until Jesus comes!

The financial increase God wants to entrust to you is so much more than you can even dream, think, or imagine. But you'll never see it until you sow seed as a lifestyle.

What Does It Take?

Back in Jesus' day, a sower didn't have all the heavy farm equipment farmers own today. The sower had to get down on his knees in order to sow his seed. He'd clear the ground, plant some seed, and then move forward a little bit. Then he'd clear another patch of ground, plant some more seed, and move on a little farther. He'd keep looking for new places to plant until all of his seed had been sown.

That's what you have to do as a sower—you continually look for ways to *give* in a world that is continually finding ways to *get*. Instead of hoarding and gathering up for yourself, you make a daily practice of looking for new places to sow.

For instance, the house I'm living in is completely paid for. "That's because God has blessed you, Nasir," you say. But why has He been able to bless my family? Because God gave seed to my wife, Anita, and me that we then sowed into others' lives.

You see, Anita and I helped six people with down payments on their houses. What were we doing? Sowing. What was the harvest? Our own home is completely paid off. That is a manifestation of God's principles at work in the earth!

Don't Let Material Things Have *You*

You see, when sowing is more important to you than hoarding material possessions, God will find ways to bless you with those possessions. Remember, He doesn't have a problem with your having things; He has a problem with things having *you*.

How do you know when something has you? When you're not ready to give it away even if God asks you to, then you know. In fact, if something you own is so precious that you're not willing to sow it, I question the depth of your trust in the Lord. What exactly is so valuable in your life that you can't part with it because you're afraid God won't replenish it?

"Lord, I'll sow anything but that...and that...and that." Oh, really? I thought you loved and trusted Jesus!

"Oh, Lord, not that dress. I'll give any other one, but that's my favorite!" Look out! The Lord will probably tell you to give that dress away, because that's the dress that has you.

But when you catch the spirit of prosperity, you'll suddenly realize there isn't one thing you own so big and valuable which God can't replace with better and more.

I know a young couple who learned that hard lesson through their attachment to their beautiful, four-thousand-square-foot home. The couple loved their home, but maintaining it and paying taxes on it had become more and more expensive.

Finally, it came to the point that the husband and wife couldn't afford to keep the house. But instead of selling it, they looked for other ways to cut back, even sacrificing certain basic needs in order to keep their house.

But one day they finally realized, "We don't own this house—this house owns *us!*" So they let go of it in their hearts and sold it.

From that day on, the couple's life changed. They've seen miracle after miracle in the financial realm. Everything has fallen into place for them, because that house and other material things don't have them bound anymore.

When owning a big house is no big deal to you, you'll own one. When driving a new car is no big deal, you'll drive one.

But don't go looking for those blessings. Just get busy sowing the way God wants you to, and the blessings will hunt you down.

I'm telling you, you can't out-give God, because God's very nature is that of a sower. He sowed His very best—His only Son. God's a Sower, and He's looking for those who will manifest His nature on this earth.

"But I'm not a giver," you may say. Oh, yes, you are! The very Spirit of giving inhabits the inside of you, and therefore, that facet of God's nature makes up a part of your recreated spirit.

Of course, you may choose not to manifest the Spirit of giving. But when you stand before Jesus at the end of your life, you won't be able to protest, "I just wasn't a natural giver, Jesus. I couldn't become the kind of sower You wanted me to be, so I didn't sow anything and stayed broke."

Jesus would respond, "Oh, yes, the Spirit of giving did dwell within you. You just decided not to develop it."

God Provides Seed to the Sower

It's so important to become a sower because that's the only way you'll receive seed to sow!

And [God] Who provides seed for the sower and bread for eating will also provide and multiply your [resources for] sowing, and increase the fruits of your righteousness [which manifests itself in active goodness, kindness and charity].
—2 Corinthians 9:10

Notice that God isn't in the *harvest-giving* business; He's in the *seed-giving* business. And He doesn't scatter seed to every Christian; He provides seed for the *sower*—the one God finds continually on his knees, looking for places to sow.

If you tell me that God has never provided seed for you, then only two possibilities exist for you: Number one, maybe you're not a sower. Number two, maybe you're eating your seed.

You see, God doesn't sit in heaven, selecting the believers He likes best so He can give only them seed. No, He looks for one thing: those who will sow the seed He provides.

Why does God look for sowers? Because seed in the hands of one who doesn't sow can never grow to its full potential for that person or for the Gospel.

Think of it this way. Imagine that you are God, sitting up in heaven with a big bag of seed ready to distribute. Would you give that seed to someone who stores or squanders it, or would you search for someone who plants that seed, expecting a harvest? You'd give seed to the *sower!*

God gives; He doesn't withhold. And when He sees that you're living the lifestyle of a sower, He will find ways to get seed into your hand. Seed will hunt you down! Why? Because God knows that if He can get money *to* you as a sower, He'll get it *through* you.

But many times when God provides seed, people don't correctly identify it as seed. They think, *Well, I needed the six blessings I just received. But after I get the seventh blessing, I'll use that as my seed.* But people who think that way don't realize that the first six blessings they received may have actually been their seed!

If you learn to correctly identify it, you'll see that God has many ways of providing seed. For example, maybe you made some money from a garage sale of things you don't use anymore. Well, did you ever think about asking God whether or not the money you made is seed He provided?

You see, you don't know what the future will bring, but God does. He knows what you're going to need in three months, in six months, and in a year from now, and that's why He wants you to sow toward your harvest.

What Hinders the Harvest?

One day I asked the Lord, "Lord, I don't understand. Why are so many Christians broke? Why isn't there more of a harvest in the body of Christ?"

The Lord replied, "Son, it isn't an issue of harvest; it's always an issue of *seedtime*. Seed just isn't getting planted."

He continued, "If men and women would trust Me enough to start planting seed for their harvest, I could give them the harvest they desire."

People who don't trust God to meet their needs fall right into the enemy's trap. Afraid they won't have enough for themselves, they gather and heap up seed, keeping it stored away in their storehouses, or banks. And since their seed never gets planted, the seed itself remains all the harvest they ever reap. And then they wonder why God seems to pass them by at harvesttime!

But no successful farmer keeps his seed locked away in a barn, because he knows that storing seed in a barn never produced a harvest.

Someone might say, "But I'm believing God that I'll have enough not only to pay off my mortgage, but to make investments in some mutual funds and term deposits for my retirement. I won't be able to do that if I give all my surplus away!"

It's not wrong to invest in mutual funds or term deposits. But always remember that *God* is your Provider and your

All-Sufficiency, and don't let your faith rest in mutual funds and term deposits rather than in Him.

You see, money only contains value to God when it is turned into goods and services that help people. Money heaped up in a bank account doesn't bless or prosper anyone, nor does it get the Gospel out or help people get saved, healed, delivered, and set free.

Think about it. What are you going to do when Jesus returns—grab your bank statement and say, "Okay, let's go"?

I don't think so! But money sown into the kingdom will reap a harvest of redeemed souls who will follow you to heaven. After all, how much of the earthly wealth you've gathered and heaped up for yourself can you take with you when Jesus comes? Absolutely, none.

"That's pretty radical, Nasir. Are you telling me to give away everything I have?" No, of course you do need to maintain a bank account and such. But I *am* telling you to be willing to give whatever God asks you to give—because if you don't, He can't get more to you.

So if you want to be a good steward of your money, don't tell me how much you have stored up in your bank account. That won't tell me anything except that you may not be listening to God! Instead, show me how God is leading you to plant and sow.

Another strategy the devil uses to hinder people's harvest is doubt and unbelief. Often believers give up too soon. They get weary as they wait and wait and no harvest comes. So just as the harvest is breaking loose for them, they become frustrated and change their confession from words of faith to words of doubt and unbelief.

They may say, "Years ago, I planted that seed over there, but I never reaped any harvest from it. So I'm giving up on this sowing business—it just doesn't work."

Oh, really? You're saying that God's law of sowing and reaping doesn't work?

"Well," these people say, "sometimes it works, and sometimes it doesn't. You never really know."

Are you calling God a liar? "No, I wouldn't do that," they argue. "I just don't believe in seedtime and harvest." But saying that is the same as calling God a liar, because He's the One who set that law in motion!

Those people should read what the Bible says about a double-minded man. James wrote to the church, "If I see you doubting, I'm going to sit you down and tell you not to expect anything from God because you're like a wave, tossed to and fro by the wind" (James 1:6,7).

How about you? Are you a believer or a doubter when it comes to looking to God for your needs to be met? To locate yourself, think about the kind of words that come out of your mouth.

Maybe you'd say something like, "Yes, I believe God's Word will work because the preacher said so. But I might not believe it tomorrow because look what happened last year— my prayer didn't get answered. Oh, I don't know. Maybe the Word will work, or maybe it won't."

But those are the words of a doubter! And if you keep wavering between faith in God's kingdom principles and your own fleshly doubts, don't be surprised if your harvest doesn't come in. Either you believe God's Word or you don't, but you can't waver and still receive your harvest.

If you've planted seed, don't give up on it too soon because of doubt and unbelief. Your harvest may be just about to arrive!

Satan's Number-One Hindrance To Reaping a Harvest: *Fear*

Doubt and unbelief in God's Word cause people to fall prey to Satan's number-one strategy for keeping God's people in financial bondage: fear.

Many times when the Holy Spirit nudges someone to sow some seed, they think, *If I give that money away, I might not have enough for my own needs. I may not even have enough to eat!*

But that is a lie from the pit of hell! A statement like that tells me that you don't know God's character. God is a God of love. So don't worry. God will see to it that there is plenty left over to meet your needs as you faithfully sow the seed He's provided for you.

The Psalmist David said he had never seen the righteous forsaken nor God's children begging for bread (Psalm 37:25). And you are not going to be God's first exception!

God promises to give you everything you need, but the enemy whispers to people's minds, "You won't have enough for tomorrow. You better hang on to your money, because if you give it away, you'll be broke tomorrow."

Or the devil will say, "You're going to do *what* with your last hundred dollars? Give it to the church? You're crazy! You and your pillow are going to sleep on the street tomorrow night! All of your neighbors will laugh at you, and you'll die of starvation."

Many Christians listen to the enemy and then reason to themselves, "I must make sure I have enough for the rent next week, so I better not sow this money now," or "This is my last twenty dollars; I better not give this."

Or someone who just lost his job may think, *I was a giver when I had a job. But since I don't receive a paycheck every Friday anymore, I'm going to hang on to my savings.*

No, that's how the world thinks. But remember, God said, **"My thoughts are not your thoughts"** (Isaiah 55:8).

Your job is not your source; *God* is. Therefore, your giving should not be totally dependent on a predictable source of income. God's source of supply never runs out, so what are you worried about?

God knit you together in your mother's womb. He gave you the very breath that keeps you alive today. His love for you is so strong that it endures forever—so strong, in fact, that He gave His only Son to die on the Cross for you. And He now calls you His child!

Your Father will provide for you. Even an earthly father makes sure his children are fed and taken care of, so how much more will your Heavenly Father take care of you (Matthew 7:11)?

Remember also that God said, "I'll never leave you nor forsake you" (Hebrews 13:5). In troubled times, He promises to always be there, always provide for you, bless you, cause your business to prosper, and give you pay increases, supernatural favor, and inspired ideas.

In every area of life, God wants to stand by you—if you'll only trust Him and sow seed as He directs you.

But the enemy doesn't want you to think this way or to trust in your Heavenly Father, so he uses fear to stop you from planting your seed. The devil knows that if he can get you to keep your seed in your pocketbook or in your bank account, he can keep you broke. As long as he can keep you from putting your seed in the ground, he won't have any problem with your harvest because there won't *be* any!

Harvest never comes until you first sow. So as long as the enemy can keep you wrapped up in fear about giving, you might as well hang on to the little you have instead of haphazardly tossing it into the offering as some sort of "tip" to God. God doesn't need your tip. In fact, if you're only tipping Him, I suggest you keep your money—you're going to need it!

You see, unless you sow seed deliberately to God, you can't expect a harvest. And that's difficult to do when the devil's got you bound by fear.

Do you know what I do when the enemy tells me, "You're not going to have enough if you give"? I laugh! "Ha, ha, ha!" I say, "I'm not going to have enough? Satan, if you don't be quiet, I'm going to double this check!"

That scares him, because he knows the law of sowing and reaping exists on this planet, and he wants to do everything he can to stop me from operating in it. He'll do the same to you, but only if you allow it.

Jesus shared this kingdom mystery so we could get serious about sowing. It isn't something we should play around with. It is time for us to stop being satisfied with the little offerings we arbitrarily give here and there, until we're good stewards of our seeds, we'll never see the supernatural increase we desire.

It's up to you. If you don't overcome fear, the enemy can keep you broke all your life. But you don't have to let the enemy control your harvest anymore through the fear of not having enough. You can trust in God, remembering that He not only gives seed to the sower, but bread for the eating (2 Corinthians 9:10). And His supply never runs out!

God knows that you need to eat and drink. He knows *all* of your needs. So don't worry about them. God will make sure your needs are met as you apply the kingdom secret of sowing to your life. Because when you get ahold of the truth of this mystery, it will break that curse of poverty over your life completely and forever!

Chapter 8
Seedtime and Harvest

While the earth remaineth, seedtime and harvest, and cold and heat, and summer and winter, and day and night shall not cease.

—Genesis 8:22 KJV

The law of seedtime and harvest is one of the unchanging principles God set in place to govern this universe. It is a law that operates in people's lives for blessing as they apply it to their lives and sow good seed. Inevitably, that good seed becomes a harvest, according to the law of seedtime and harvest.

God Looks for Channels

If you want to experience the blessings of seedtime and harvest for yourself, it's time to change your thinking to that of a sower's mentality. Shake yourself and say, "Hey, wait a minute! Lord, everything I have is Yours anyway, so I'll give whatever You tell me to."

You see, God looks for channels through which He can funnel finances for the end-time harvest, but He wants rivers that flow, not dams that stop the flow.

If you want to be one of God's channels, you will have to spend time with Him, learning to listen to His voice. As you do, He will tell you exactly where to sow.

He may point out a brother or sister in the congregation who needs financial help, or He may direct you to sow into a particular ministry that is doing a good work for His kingdom. He may also ask you to sow your compassion, your time, or your love.

Learning to know His voice in order to be a vessel of blessing comes through spending time in the Word and in prayer.

Channels for the Anointing

Because God moves through people on this earth, He is looking for channels not only for finances, but also channels for His power and anointing to flow through.

When Jesus, the Head of the church, wants something done on this earth, He directs a member of His body to do it. As the believer obeys Him, the anointing flows.

God's anointing is not meant to be kept to one's self; it's always meant to flow through you to someone else. Consider the example of Jesus. He was never anointed for His own benefit. He never said, "The Spirit of the Lord has anointed Me so I can enjoy that anointing."

No, God anointed Jesus so He could minister the anointing to others. Notice that Jesus said, "The Spirit of the Lord has anointed me to preach good news to the poor, bring sight to the blind, and set the captives free" (Luke 4:18). The anointing carries with it a *purpose*.

Sometimes I ask people why they stepped forward for prayer in a service. Some of them answer, "I want more anointing on my life."

I ask these people, "What did you do this week with the anointing that's already in you? Did you witness to anyone? Teach the Word to anyone? Lay hands on any sick people? It's great that you want more of God's anointing on your life, but what are you going to do with it?"

Often, those same people don't know what to answer. But I can ask such questions because I've had the Lord ask the same of me. Once He asked me, "Nasir, do you want more anointing in your life?"

"Yes, Lord, of course I want more!"

"Well, then," the Lord said, "start letting it flow more, and it will grow."

Like any other gift from God, His power and anointing increases as it flows out of you. The more you allow His power to flow *out of* you, the more God's power will flow *into* you.

It's the same way with finances. The more you allow your finances to flow out of you, the more God will bless you with finances to flow to and through you.

Turn on the Tap!

Think, for example, about the water faucet in your home. The tap connects to a pipe, and the pipe links up to the water system in your town.

When you want a glass of water, you simply walk to the sink, turn on the tap, and let the water flow out. You are the one who determines whether the water flows out in a trickle or a flood.

Now where was the water just before you turned on the tap? In the reservoir? No, it was in the pipe. The water flowing out of the tap is immediately replenished by water from the city into your pipe. And if the tap is only opened a little, only a small amount of water needs replenishing.

That's what seedtime and harvest is like. Think of yourself as the pipe and that water as both your seed and harvest. If you want a big harvest, remember, you're the one who controls the flow, so open the tap more!

You determine the size of your harvest; the enemy doesn't. He never has. In fact, your financial increase doesn't depend on anyone but you.

If you only allow the water to drip, drip, drip out of the tap, then the water to replace the outflow can only flow back at the same rate, "drip, drip, drip." To change that, just turn on the tap until it's a floodgate!

You don't have to worry—the "pipe" will never run empty, because God wants to flood water through it to you. But He can't replenish your supply until you empty yourself of what you already have.

The control to the faucet is in your hands. *You* decide if you're going to open it for a trickle or a flood. And if you allow God to flow *through* you, He will always find a way to get blessings *to* you!

Your Heavenly Father's Supply
Never Runs Out

Most people don't allow themselves to be God's channels simply because they don't know by revelation their Supplier's character. But here's what the Bible says:

116

☐ Yes! I would like to receive the free teaching tape on miracles and additional information on your books and teaching series.

(Please Print)

Title:

Name:

Address:

Apt. #/Suite #:

City:

State/Province:

Zip/Postal Code:

Country:

Home Phone:

Work Phone:

Cell Phone:

Email:

Please detach along preforation.

Free Tape!

"RELEASING YOUR MIRACLE"

Please detach and mail.

www.wisdomministries.org

BUSINESS REPLY MAIL

FIRST-CLASS MAIL   PERMIT NO. 17551   BROKEN ARROW OK

POSTAGE WILL BE PAID BY ADDRESSEE

WISDOM MINISTRIES INC

PO BOX 2720
BROKEN ARROW OK 74013-9906

As for the rich in this world, charge them not to be proud and arrogant and contemptuous of others, nor to set their hopes on uncertain riches, but on GOD, WHO RICHLY AND CEASELESSLY PROVIDES US WITH EVERYTHING FOR [OUR] ENJOYMENT.

[Charge them] to do good, to be rich in good works, to be liberal and generous of heart, ready to share [with others].

—1 Timothy 6:17-18

I wrote in the margin of my Bible next to this passage, "Give, and believe God that there is no end to His supply." Never-ending supply is God's promise in these verses.

When my son, Matthew, was five years old, he started doing something which really strengthened my trust in my Heavenly Father as a faithful Provider.

Matthew couldn't conceive that there might ever be a shortage of toys. Therefore, when he went to school, he often gave away one of his toys to someone in his class.

I wondered, *What am I supposed to tell Matthew—that there is a shortage of toys and he shouldn't give away so freely what is his?*

No, I couldn't do that, because Matthew knows his daddy loves him and would never allow him to run out of toys. In fact, his daddy wanted to give him even more toys as a reward for learning to share!

That's the way you should trust your Heavenly Father to supply your needs. First, realize that His supply literally cannot run out. As we've already read, He owns the cattle on a thousand hills (Psalm 50:10) and He also owns every gold, silver, and diamond mine on the planet. He owns every sun, star, moon, and planet in the universe. It's obvious that it's impossible for God's supply to run out.

Second, understand that because you are intimately connected to a Father whose supply never runs out, He will always provide you with seed to sow.

So that's what I mean when I say that learning to live by the law of seedtime and harvest is really just a matter of getting to know your Heavenly Father. When you know Him, you realize His mighty arms of protection and provision surround you at all times. You understand that He will always be there to supply your every need.

Don't Set Your Hopes On Uncertain Riches

I want to show you something else about God's abundance. Let's look back at our text in First Timothy 6. Verse 17 says: **"As for the rich in this world, charge them not to be proud and arrogant and contemptuous of others, nor to set their hopes on uncertain riches, but on God, Who richly and ceaselessly provides us with everything for [our] enjoyment."**

This passage refers to two kinds of riches. The first are called uncertain riches; the second are the riches God gives us.

How do you tell the difference between the two? That's easy. Uncertain riches are what I call "stacked-up" riches, or riches that a person gathers and heaps up for himself because his trust is in money. But God's riches are *given*.

"Well," some people say, "I stack up money for those unexpected 'rainy days' when an emergency hits." But if you keep stacking up your wealth rather than using some of it as seed, you'll spend your whole life having rainy days because that's what you sowed to! That's exactly why stacked-up wealth is uncertain.

For instance, look at the many rich people in the world. Often their trust is in their "stack." They buy surveillance video cameras and guard dogs; they build walls and hire security guards—all because they're afraid someone will steal the riches they've heaped up!

God doesn't have any problem with your having riches as long as you're willing to give when He tells you to. And having that willingness is only a matter of trusting Him that His supply never runs out. You see, *faith freely gives, but fear holds on.*

It set me free when I learned to trust in my Heavenly Father to meet all of my needs. Now I don't care about hoarding my stack. My stack isn't mine anyway; it's His.

And if my Father wants to use that stack to help someone, that's fine with me. I found out that if I'm faithful to give with a little stack, God will trust me with a bigger stack.

And what can He trust me to do with that bigger stack? The same thing I did with the smaller one—sow it whenever He tells me to! The key to living God's abundant life is following the law of seedtime and harvest.

The Riches God Gives Us To Enjoy

The second kind of riches are given to us by God, **"Who richly and ceaselessly provides us with everything for [our] enjoyment"** (First Timothy 6:17).

God wants us to have a good time! But the key to enjoying all the things He gives us is to be ready to give them away. God charges those to whom He gives His abundance **"...to be rich in good works, to be liberal and generous of heart, ready to share [with others]"** (v. 18).

"But how can I enjoy my material possessions if I'm always giving them away?" you ask. That's the whole point—you actually find joy in giving them!

"God gave me this car," someone boasts. Great! But to truly enjoy it, be ready to give what God has given you. That's catching the spirit of prosperity.

Some people think the object of prosperity is to "get, get, get." But it's actually to "give, give, give." You have to become a giver, not a getter, so you can be a reaper, not a keeper!

If God tells you to give away your brand-new car, take a deep breath and give it! The car manufacturers build more each year, and the next model is even better!

Get to know your Daddy in heaven, trust in His everlasting supply, and you'll have no problem with giving. In fact, you'll grow to the place where you find greater pleasure in giving than you do in receiving.

If you only have ten dollars in your pocket and your Heavenly Father tells you, "Give your ten dollars to that person over there," you won't even think twice about it; you will just obey. If He tells you to give your best suit away, you'll do it in a heartbeat—with *joy*.

When you know your Father, you can live a continually fulfilled life whether you are abased or you abound. God gives to you richly to enjoy, you learn how enjoyable it is to give as well!

Freely Share of Your Substance

As a father of three sons, I've learned so much about the heart of my Heavenly Father. For example, in my efforts to teach my own children how to share, I've come to realize how much God wants His children to learn the same lesson. That's why in 1 Timothy 6:18 He gives us a fatherly exhortation, telling us to be ready always to share with others.

For Anita and me, teaching our youngest sons to share with each other hasn't always been easy. Because our son Matthew is three years older than Josiah, most of the toys belonged to him first. So when Josiah comes into the playroom, Matthew wants to lay claim to his "territory."

Here's a standard scenario. Matthew will grab several toys and retreat to a corner. There he stands in front of the toys, guarding them from his little brother. When Josiah comes over and tries to pick up one of Matthew's toys, Matthew protests, "No, I got them first!"

As a father, it grieves me to see my son act selfishly. I sit him down and tell him, "No, son, don't be like that. You need to share with your brother."

How much more then is our Father in heaven grieved when we act selfishly with our earthly possessions? How much more does He want us to learn to share freely with one another?

God wants us to share freely of our substance. I believe God's message of giving is this: "I bless you with finances, but not for you to just store them away for yourself. Share with your brothers and sisters in Christ!"

It shouldn't be hard for us to imagine that our Father would want that from us. After all, He is the Author of giving and was in fact the first ever to share. He could have kept this universe to Himself, but He decided to share it with you and me.

Do you remember what happened in the book of Acts? The believers all shared their substance with each other, and the church exploded (Acts 2:44,45). The church prospered as they finally got a revelation of seedtime and harvest and became God's channels of blessing. They learned to share what God had so richly given them to enjoy.

It's Not How Much You Give, But How Much Is Left Over

Some people come to church, and when the offering plate goes by, they put in the smallest bill they can find in their wallet.

That doesn't please God, He doesn't care how much you give; His concern is how much you have left over.

You see, if you only have one hundred dollars to your name and you give fifty dollars, that's a big deal to God. But if you have ten thousand dollars in the bank and you give fifty dollars, that's a different story. You may not have the spirit of giving!

Don't Value Money More Than People

Christians sometimes fail to share their uncertain riches because fear, the enemy's number-one strategy, makes them value money more than the goods and services it can buy to help people. In essence, they value money *over* people.

Often, a person who yields to fear is only interested in seeing his bank account balance increase. He gives more value to that balance than to what his money can buy to bless others.

The moment money becomes more important to a person than helping others, that person yields to the deceitfulness of riches and the father of fear then begins to guide him.

First, the enemy tells him to stack up riches for himself. If the person allows it, the devil eventually leads him to the very root of evil; the love of money. That person will serve mammon, not God, because he cannot serve two masters.

What a dangerous progression! But it all starts by valuing money more than people.

On the other hand, when you value people more than the money you can accumulate, you actually manifest the nature of God and catch the spirit of prosperity.

God is pleased when we value people enough to share freely with them *today*, trusting Him to supply our every need *tomorrow*.

Imagine this scene by way of illustration: Say I walk into the kitchen, and my youngest son Josiah says he can't find the box of breakfast cereal. As we search the house, we discover it under my other son Matthew's bed. So I ask Matthew, "Son, why do you have the cereal box under your bed?"

"I'm hanging on to it, Daddy, and no one else can have any."

"But, why?"

"Because I don't know if you'll buy cereal for me tomorrow, so I'm hiding this box safe under my bed for me."

That kind of situation seems so ridiculous, doesn't it? Actually, the opposite is true at my house. All of my sons run to the refrigerator and eat whenever they're hungry, and none of them hide food away for themselves. They never once say, "I wonder if we'll have enough for tomorrow."

My sons don't lose one bit of sleep wondering if there will be food in the refrigerator tomorrow, because they know that the same father who put food there that day is the same father who puts food there the next day.

My sons implicitly trust their father to be a faithful supplier of their every need, so they have no problem sharing among themselves. How much more should we likewise allow ourselves to be God's channels, valuing each other enough to freely share of our substance as we trust Him to faithfully supply all of our needs?

I'm convinced that there is a lot more money in the body of Christ than we know of. The problem is, too many Christians value money over people, and they keep their riches stored away! They hide away seed in "barns" when it's meant to flow back and forth among God's people, meeting needs and getting the Gospel out to the ends of the earth!

A Lesson in Being God's Channel of Blessing

I myself have had many opportunities to learn to be a willing channel for God's blessings to flow through. For example, while I was a Bible college student, I worked as an usher at the church. When the church services concluded, I always stood at the back of the auditorium and shook hands with people as they left.

On one of those occasions, as a man stopped to shake my hand, he slipped a piece of paper into my palm and said, "Bless you, brother" and then just walked away.

It crossed my mind that the man may have given me some money, but I was too busy ushering; I couldn't look at it. So I put the folded piece of paper in my pocket and continued to shake hands with others who were leaving the service.

It wasn't until later that I remembered to pull out the piece of paper and look at it. It was a one-hundred-dollar bill!

I said, "Glory, hallelujah! This is wonderful! Someone just walked up to me and gave me a hundred dollars! I can't wait to get home and tell Anita about this!"

That afternoon I had to go to another appointment and then on to usher at a night service before I went home. Before the service began, I stood at my post in the back of the sanctuary and watched people start trickling in.

Suddenly the Spirit of God spoke up on the inside of me. "Do you see that man sitting over by the wall, seven rows back?" He asked.

I looked over and saw the man the Lord was talking about. "Yes, Lord, I do," I replied.

"Give him the hundred dollars."

What? I thought, *Give away the hundred-dollar bill I just received? Satan, I rebuke you! This can't be God. I've already planned out how I'm going to spend that money!*

I had planned to pay my ten-dollar tithe, give a ten-dollar offering, and then use the rest of the money for some of the family's basic needs. Eighty dollars can go a long way for a full-time Bible school student with a wife and three children!

But the Spirit of God continued, "No, this is Me. Give the one hundred dollars to that man."

"Lord, I haven't even shown this money to my wife. Can't I just show it to her?"

"No, give the money now."

I sighed and said, "All right, Lord." So I walked over to this man whom I had never met in my life, and said, "All I can tell you is that God loves you, and He's going to see you through."

Then as I shook the man's hand, I transferred the hundred-dollar bill from my hand to his and walked away. When I glanced back, the man was overcome with emotion and close to tears.

To this day I have no idea who that man was or what problem he faced in his life. It's none of my business; I was just a vessel.

But I can tell you this: *God* knew, and He also knew what that man needed. And God wanted *me* to learn how to be a lifestyle sower, a channel through which He could freely flow to bless and help others.

So if you want to see blessings flowing into your life, learn to obey God's voice when He tells you to sow seed.

Remember, Deuteronomy 28:1 says that if you listen to the voice of the Lord and do all that is written in His Word, all of God's blessings will come upon you and overtake you. But unless you're willing to obey His voice, blessings won't overtake you.

You see, God is orchestrating a master plan. He sees one of His children going through a tough time financially, and He also sees one of His other children with the finances to help. Therefore, He prompts the child who possesses more to give to the child experiencing lack. Thus both believers are blessed—one in his giving and the other in his receiving.

But God can't use you in His grand master plan if you won't listen for His voice. In fact, He'll have to pass you by and go on to plan B. And if the person to be the channel of blessing in plan B doesn't listen, God will go on to plan C.

One way or another, God *will* meet that need. But you will be the person who loses the most if you don't hearken unto His voice or obey His Word by sowing.

There's another chapter to that hundred-dollar story. Before I left the service that night, someone I barely knew came up to me and handed me an envelope. I thanked him and left for home without opening it, intent on telling my wife about my experience with the hundred-dollar bill. (At least I could tell the story, even though I couldn't spend the money!)

As I was relating to Anita what had happened, she opened the envelope I'd gotten just before coming home. Inside a card was a check for three hundred and fifty dollars!

No one will ever convince me that I didn't receive that money because of my obedience to sow first that hundred-dollar bill.

"But why didn't God simply send the man who had the hundred dollars to the man in the night service who needed it?" you ask. Well, He could have, but if He had, *I* would have missed the blessing of sowing into that stranger's life and reaping a harvest!

So why does God give something to you only to have you turn around and give it to someone else? He does it to bless you as well. That's the fun of being one of His channels of blessing!

The Power in a Seed

What if God wants to use *you* as a channel the way He used me with the hundred-dollar-bill? Does the thought of giving away all the financial increase you just received scare you a little? If it does, you simply need to get a revelation of the awesome power in a seed.

You see, a seed contains the power and potential to multiply. In itself, it doesn't look like much, but when planted, that little seed carries enough power to shoot roots deep into the ground. You and I may need the aid of a shovel to dig into the ground, but a seed needs no force other than itself.

And as the roots dig down, there's still ample power in that seed to push a tiny plant out of its shell upward, fighting its way up through the soil until it finally pushes through to the open air.

Where did the power come from—power enough to cause both the roots to shoot down and the plant to push up through the soil? That power comes from the seed itself.

Next the fledgling plant thickens into a stalk; then the stalk grows leaves and finally bears fruit. And within that fruit dwells many, many, many more seeds full of the same power and potential of the initial seed—a multiplied harvest!

One day as I was driving to Branson, Missouri, I saw places along the highway where road crews literally dynamited through huge rocks in order to create the road. At one such place I looked up and saw a little tree growing on the side of one of those rocks.

I thought, *How in the world did that tree ever have the might, strength, and energy to kick and fight its way through that rock, shooting its roots down so it could grow?* And I realized the incredible power that resides within the seed of one tree!

A Seed Unplanted Yields No Harvest

Jesus tells us that the power and potential in a seed will never be brought forth if left unplanted. The harvest dies within the seed, wasted.

I assure you, most solemnly I tell you, Unless a grain of wheat falls into the earth and dies, it remains [just one grain; it never becomes more but lives] by itself alone. But if it dies, it produces many others and yields a rich harvest.

—John 12:24

Once again, Jesus gives the disciples another kingdom principle, but this time He starts off by saying, "I assure you, most solemnly I tell you." In other words, He's saying, "I tell you the truth."

Now Jesus always told the truth, and the disciples knew that. But He wanted to shake the disciples up a little and make them pay attention. So He essentially said, "Listen up—what I'm about to tell you is crucial!"

What kingdom principle did Jesus consider so important? Simply this: A seed unplanted contains power and potential. *But it never exercises that power and potential unless it is planted in the ground.*

God provides seed to you if you are a sower. But until that seed gets planted in the ground, He won't be able to **"...multiply your [resources for] sowing"** (2 Corinthians 9:10).

Notice that God will multiply your *sowing*. If you aren't sowing, He has nothing to multiply.

You see, God doesn't even need to concern Himself with multiplying your harvest; as you plant the seed, it *automatically* multiplies! The seed multiplies independently because seedtime and harvest is a law that governs this earth. If you plant seed, you *will* see a harvest.

God *is* interested in multiplying His people's *sowing*. If He can get His children to sow more, the harvests will take care of themselves. God wants to bring a mighty harvest to the body of Christ, but the only way He can is through His own law of seedtime and harvest. That's why He wants you to sow seed.

Someone may say, "I'm broke. I have a need." God's answer is simple: "Plant a seed, My child. I already put My laws on the earth, so start operating in those laws. Be a sower, for *from a seed unplanted your only harvest will be a seed.*"

The problem with too many Christians is that they live on seed instead of living on harvest.

God says to a believer, "Three of My children are struggling because they can't pay their bills, and you have all this money stored up in your bank account. Why don't you share out of your abundance?"

"But, Lord, that's my nest egg!"

"Child, I'm not trying to *take* your nest egg," he prods, "I'm trying to *increase* it. And the reason it hasn't increased before now is that your 'nest egg' is actually your seed and you never planted it. Therefore, your seed has become the extent of your harvest!"

If you have ten dollars in your pocket and you don't plant it, then that ten dollars is all the harvest you'll have. But if you sow your ten dollars into the kingdom, God can multiply your sowing and bring the harvest of that seed back to you.

So obey the voice of the Lord when He tells you to sow. If what you have isn't enough to meet your need, chances are it's intended to be used as a seed!

But remember, only seed that's in the ground can grow. You may not be able to multiply what you hold in your hand, but God can—if you plant it. He's the God of multiplication!

The Power To Multiply
In a Kernel of Corn

Let's look at the development of a kernel of corn as a graphic illustration of the awesome potential contained in one seed. You couldn't get too full from eating one small kernel of corn, could you? You might put a little salt and butter on it and try to savor it for a moment, but you'd leave the table as hungry as you came.

But what would happen if you planted that same kernel in the ground? A friend of mine did the math on that and told me that the average kernel produces one stalk with two cobs of corn. Each ear of corn produces an average of 452 kernels. That's a total of 904 kernels from just one small kernel planted in the ground!

Now you could cook those two cobs and eat those 904 kernels, and they would probably taste great and satisfy your hunger for a few hours. But if you had the mentality of a sower you'd think, *Wow! If one kernel could produce this many more kernels, I think I'll take these 904 kernels and plant them again!*

If you plant those 904 kernels they will multiply into a harvest of 746,496 kernels of corn! That's three-quarters of a million kernels harvested from one kernel by sowing the increase just once. You've tapped into the powerful law of seedtime and harvest!

God is the One who put the law of increase into effect on this earth. Do you think He would make that law more effective for corn than He would for planting into His kingdom? No way! And like anything else we've discussed, the law of seedtime and harvest is even more real in the spiritual realm than it is in the natural realm.

We limit God when we say, "I want a hundredfold return on my giving, Lord." The God of too much must say, "But what's wrong with four hundredfold? Or how about if I were to give you a thousandfold? Do you have any problem with that?"

The Lord told me long ago, "Son, your faith limits Me." Ever since then, I've said, "Okay, Lord, I'm taking the roof off my faith. No more limits!"

So don't be afraid to sow seed, but believe in the power of the seed to multiply. God will never tell you to do something that will hurt you. He wants you to plant seed because He's trying to get a blessing to you. You see, God has a great harvest prepared, and He's ready to pour more blessings into your life—but it's up to you to tap into the power of the seed!

Elijah and the Widow

Let's look at the biblical account of the prophet Elijah and the widow of Zarephath to see how the God of multiplication works. (1 Kings 17:5-16.)

The people of Gilead experienced a great drought in the land. Elijah had been staying near the brook Cherith at the Lord's command. There God had supernaturally provided His prophet with food, sending ravens to bring him bread and meat.

But when the brook dried up because of the drought, God gave Elijah new instructions: **"Arise, go to Zarephath, which belongs to Sidon, and dwell there. Behold, I have commanded a widow there to provide for you"** (v. 9).

So Elijah obeyed the Lord and traveled to Zarephath. He found the widow God told him about out gathering sticks, and asked her to bring him some water. As she went to get it, Elijah said, **"Bring me a morsel of bread in your hand"** (v. 11).

It was no little thing for Elijah to ask this widow to bring him a morsel of bread since bread was scarce and worth a lot of money during the time of famine! Nevertheless, Elijah told the woman, "Bring the morsel to me. Plant it into my ministry."

We can see from verse 9 that God had already commanded this woman to feed Elijah before he'd ever arrived. But obviously, she wasn't planning on obeying. She told Elijah: **As the Lord your God lives, I have not a loaf baked but only a handful of meal in the jar and a little oil in the bottle. See, I am gathering two sticks, that I may go in and bake it for me and my son, that we may eat it, and die** (v. 12).

(Now don't judge this woman too quickly. How many times has God spoken to *you* about sowing seed and you weren't obedient!)

The widow operated in fear—the fear of not having enough. She got so busy looking at what was in her hand that she couldn't conceive of the possibility that God could take her seed and multiply it back to her as harvest.

Sounds like a familiar problem, doesn't it? We sometimes sit in church and pray, "Lord, I know I have a twenty-dollar bill in my pocket. But if I give all of it in the offering now, what am I going to do for money next week?" We forget that He is El Shaddai, the God of more than enough!

This widow was saying the same thing to Elijah: "This portion of meal is all I have; this is my security." But what security did that tiny amount of meal and oil actually provide her? None! Without God's help, she was going to die anyway.

Now consider this. Could God have taken care of His man another way? Sure, He could have. God has many ways to take care of His ministers. He wasn't hard up for the widow's little bit of bread; He could have called in more ravens without any problem. Then why did God tell Elijah to travel six days to find this widow—just so the prophet could take her last morsel?

But God didn't command the widow to give her last bit of food to Elijah because He couldn't find any other way to feed His man. He did it because He was trying to get a harvest of blessing to *her*!

In relating this account of Elijah and the widow, I heard a minister once say, "Can you imagine the newspaper headlines if a reporter got ahold of a story like this one? 'Corrupt Minister Takes Widow's Last Meal.' I can just hear the public outcry, 'Jail him! Crucify him! He took that poor lady's last meal!'"

But thank God, we're not moved by the media, but only by the Word of God! The world doesn't understand how God operates. They don't understand the kingdom way of doing things. You see, there wasn't any shame in Elijah's eating the widow's last meal. In fact, his request actually gave her the opportunity to reap the harvest she so desperately needed.

The truth is, if the widow hadn't obeyed God and fed Elijah, we wouldn't be reading about her in the Bible today. She and her son would have eaten their last meal and then died, just as she feared.

But the widow did obey God—after she first told Elijah, "I have just enough meal to feed one adult and one child. If I make a cake for you first, there goes the adult portion. Logic dictates that I would only have enough left for my child."

But Elijah responded, "Don't be afraid. Just make me a little cake first, and afterwards prepare some for yourself and your son" (v. 13).

"What?" she could have said, "Elijah, you must not be listening! I just told you I have enough in my hand for only one adult and child, and you're still telling me to fix enough food for two adults and one child. Can't you count, Elijah? It isn't going to work!"

If the woman had responded that way to Elijah's request, she would have been absolutely justified. As long as she kept her eyes on what was in her hand, it never would work.

But if you give God the seed in your hand, it doesn't leave your life. God promises to multiply your sowing back into your life with the harvest He has in *His* hand.

So Elijah told the woman, *"Fear not"* (v. 13), and with those two words, he identified her problem. It's the same problem we all deal with in the area of giving—the moment God tells us to sow something, the enemy tries to bring in fear to keep us from obeying.

Then Elijah gave the reason why the widow need not fear. He shared God's promise: **"For thus says the Lord, the God of Israel, The jar of meal shall not waste away, or the bottle of oil fail, until the day that the Lord sends rain on the earth"** (v. 14).

The moment Elijah spoke those words, God's power was present for the miracle. But the woman wouldn't see her miracle unless she acted on God's Word.

At this point, the widow stood at a crossroads. It was time for her to decide, "Do I base my actions on what little I see in my hand, or do I base them on the word of the Lord?"

God required the woman to take her eyes off what she held in her hand, focus her faith on His promise to her, and sow her seed. The kingdom way *always* starts with sowing. It has to, because that is a law of the universe God set into motion before the foundations of the earth.

Do you see how much God loved this woman? He didn't need this widow's last morsel. He could have sent more ravens to feed Elijah instead. And it's not that she was the rich widow in town; she was the poorest of the poor! With only a handful of meal, she was desperate! But God said, "Even though you have little, use it to plant seed into My kingdom."

Thank God, this woman didn't go with her initial reaction of fear! She chose to believe the Word of God above what she saw in her hand, and her obedience released the financial miracle in her life. According to the word of the Lord, the meal and oil continued to multiply until the three-year drought was over!

So do you want to know how to overcome the fear of not having enough as this widow did? It's easy. The next time God asks you to sow a hundred dollars and the enemy whispers, "You aren't going to have enough for yourself," just go ahead and sow anyway!

That's how the widow of Zarephath overcame her fear— by sowing the little she had as the Lord had commanded her to do. She decided, "I choose this day to believe the word of God delivered by the prophet. I'm just going to do it!"

So when God tells you to give but the enemy says you can't afford to, just do it anyway! Check out the faithfulness of your Father, who won't fail to take care of you.

Get in the Cycle!

The moment you plant seed into God's kingdom, you enter the cycle of seedtime and harvest. The Bible describes this cycle, which operates in every realm of life:

For as the rain and snow come down from the heavens, and return not there again, but water the earth and make it bring forth and sprout, that it may give seed to the sower and bread to the eater, so shall My word be that goes forth out of My mouth.

—Isaiah 55:10,11

How does the cycle work? When you ask God for seed, He always gives you enough to start the cycle. Once you sow that, God multiplies it in order to get more seed back to you as a harvest of the seed you initially planted. Then you plant more seed, which grows and produces even more seed for you to plant again. Then the cycle repeats itself over and over and over again.

If you stay in that cycle, it will produce for you, and God will never take you out of it. Only *you* can take yourself out of the cycle of seedtime and harvest by stacking up or eating your seed—in other words, by interrupting it through not sowing seed.

I remember the day I got a deeper revelation of the law of seedtime and harvest. It was the day the Lord told me something that set me free from concerns about my finances.

You see, I travel all over the world teaching the Word. I have a wife and three sons, and we own a home, run a ministry office with staff, and oversee a thriving tape ministry—and we live by faith. No one comes looking for me at the end of the week to give me a paycheck for the work I do.

But the Lord said to me one day, "Nasir, your needs will never be met by other people giving to you."

"What do You mean, Lord?" I asked. "I'm a minister. When I travel and teach, people take up offerings for our ministry. So what do You mean, my needs aren't going to be met by people?"

The Lord replied, "Your needs won't be met by their giving. Your needs will be met by *your* giving."

That definitely got me excited about becoming more of a sower! I realized that all I need to do to increase my harvest is increase my sowing.

Since then, I've understood that it doesn't matter if I teach somewhere and only receive one dollar in the offering; I *know* my "Boss" will take care of me and my family. Because I'm a sower, I control my harvest, and whether people give or not, God guarantees my harvest!

Even as a ministry, my staff and I sow seed into the kingdom of God from every dollar that comes in. We've planted a lot of seed in the ground, and I can tell you, the law of seedtime and harvest works!

So don't miss out on the blessing—get into the cycle of seedtime and harvest and allow God to use you as a channel of blessing. The same principles of the power of the seed which work for me will work for you. If you're a sower, you have God's ironclad guarantee of a harvest!

Chapter 9
Guidelines for Sowing

"He who sows sparingly will also reap sparingly, and he who sows bountifully will also reap bountifully."

—2 Corinthians 9:6 NKJV

Now that we understand the vital role sowing plays in reaping financial prosperity and we understand the law of seedtime and harvest, we can examine the way in which we are to sow seed. The Word actually sets forth specific guidelines.

You see, sowing isn't just a matter of carelessly throwing some seed on the ground every once in a while. If you want to reap the abundant harvest God intends for you to enjoy, you must follow the guidelines for sowing that God's Word tells us about.

Sow Daily, Reap Daily

The first guideline to sowing is to do it continuously. Although the law of sowing and reaping works both in the natural and the spiritual realm, we Christians have an edge over natural sowers—farmers. You see, a farmer can plant only during the planting season, not all year round. He can't, for example, plant in the middle of winter. He has to wait for the planting season.

When that season arrives, planting, planting, planting consume the farmer's days. Even after he's planted all the seed, he waits several months more until harvest time.

But as Christians, we don't have just one planting season in which we can sow seed. In fact, it's possible to sow and reap a harvest of blessings every day of our lives!

Here's how it works. *Day 1:* My lifestyle is sowing, so guess what I'm going to do today? I'm going to sow.

Day 2: I look at my seed planted on Day 1. Nothing is happening. Do I think, *Sowing doesn't work?* No, I don't, because I understand the law of seedtime and harvest. Instead, I just sow more seed.

"But you haven't received the harvest from Day 1 yet!" you say. That's all right. Just wait and see what happens.

Day 3: Guess what I'm going to do today? Sow! "But," you say, "you haven't seen the harvest from Day 1 or Day 2 yet!" I know; just be patient, and you'll see.

Day 4: What do you think I'm going to do on Day 4? Sow. "Wait a minute—when is this harvest coming?" you keep saying. "I mean, look, you sowed on Day 1, Day 2, Day 3, and Day 4. What's going on here?" I'll tell you what's going on. I'm making sowing my lifestyle!

Day 5: What do you think I'm going to do? Sow. *Day 6:* And today? Sow. *Day 7:* Suddenly—oh, what is that? Wow! Look what I received today! Glory to Jesus, I've begun to reap a harvest! Is it a harvest from my sowing on Day 7? No, it's from Day 1! So what do you think I'm going to do now? Sow. I'm not going to allow myself to get so wrapped up in my harvest that I forget to sow!

Day 8: What do you think I do the day after I receive a harvest? I sow again! Then, look here! My goodness, another harvest! I received one yesterday, and I've received another today! This is wonderful—it's my harvest from Day 2!

Are you getting the picture? If you make sowing your daily lifestyle, you're sure to come to a place in your spiritual walk where you reap a harvest daily. That's just the inevitable outcome. Blessings will chase you down and catch up with you. Because you're so busy sowing, sowing, sowing, you'll keep on reaping harvest, harvest, harvest!

Anita and I experience that kind of daily harvest in our personal lives and in our ministry. Someone will bless us with finances, and we'll think, *Wow! Where did this harvest come from? Why would so-and-so bless us like that?*

Then the Lord reminds us, "Remember the time you planted a seed here? Or remember that other time you obeyed My voice and sowed into that person's life? Well, this is the harvest of those seeds sown."

Don't Wait for Harvest
To Sow More

Do you want to reap a harvest every day of your life? Then start sowing daily, and don't be moved by what you see.

Some people say, "I haven't seen the harvest from Day 4 yet. I think I'll just wait until I do before I sow more seed."

But let me give you an illustration to show you the folly of waiting to see harvest before you sow more seed. Have you ever seen what happens when water flowing through a pipe hits an air pocket? No more water flows out of the pipe. You have to wait until the air is expelled from the pipe before the water can flow out again.

When you don't sow daily, you create a spiritual "air pocket" in your harvest—a space of time when no harvest comes in. So if you want your harvest to continually flow, make sure you continually sow!

God Daily Loads Us With Benefits

How do we know that God wants us to enjoy a harvest every day? Because Psalm 68:19 says, **"Blessed be the Lord, WHO DAILY LOADETH US WITH BENEFITS"** (KJV).

When I first read that verse, I grabbed hold of it and said, "Hallelujah! I want daily benefits, Lord! I don't want to be limited to telling people about something that happened a year ago. In fact, I don't even want to tell people testimonies from yesterday. If I cannot experience a new testimony each day as a result of my daily sowing, then that Scripture is not working in my life!"

It's great to talk about what God did in my life ten years ago, but I want to be able to talk about what God is doing for me daily. I ought to experience God's benefits every day of my life—and so should you!

God loves to bless us with benefits both large and small. For example, I love all kinds of food, but one of the foods I enjoy the most is Japanese sushi.

One time when I was holding meetings in Toronto, Canada, I had a great desire to eat sushi. The problem was that I do not like to eat before a service, and most restaurants don't stay open late enough to eat dinner after a service. Besides that, sushi is *not* the most common menu item in Toronto restaurants.

I thought, *How will I ever find the chance to eat sushi before I leave?* So I handed it over to the Lord and forgot about it.

After one of the meetings later that week, a Filipino pastor decided to take me to a Chinese restaurant—and guess what? They had sushi on their menu! I said, "Thank You, Lord! You daily load me with benefits even in the little things!"

Start believing God for daily benefits. Wake up each morning and thank Him for the blessings you're going to receive that day. What blessings? Well, you may not know what they are at seven o'clock in the morning, but you can know that they will come before the day is over!

Therefore, if you want those daily blessings, continue to be a doer of the Word. Sow each day whether you see any harvest or not. As you do, the time will come when you experience God's benefits on a daily basis, as His Word promises.

I know this from what the Bible says: **"Give, and it shall be given unto you"** (Luke 6:38 KJV). In other words, you can count on it. You can take it to the bank. This truth is more real than the chair you're sitting in. Sow daily, and God *will* daily load you with benefits.

Don't Wait for a Surplus Before You Sow

Don't wait until you have more than you need for yourself before you sow. That's not how God's kingdom principles work.

Some people say, "When I get ten thousand dollars in the bank, then I'll give." But they probably won't. If they won't

give when they have only a little, they're decieving themselves to think they'll give when they have much.

Once those people finally obtain their ten thousand dollars (if they ever do!), they change their goal to accumulating
twenty thousand dollars in the bank before they give. Who
are they fooling?

Besides, those who say, "I'll give once I get all my
finances together" miss God's timing. Because they wait too
long to sow, they never reap the harvest that's somewhere
down the road.

The Bible teaches us that we are not to wait on surplus to
sow seed: **"He who observes the wind [and waits for all
conditions to be favorable] will not sow, and he who
regards the clouds will not reap"** (Ecclesiastes 11:4).

You can't keep your eyes on the wind, so to speak, and be
a lifestyle sower. What do I mean by that? I mean you can't
see the wind—it has no shape or color—but you can see its
effects as, for example, it blows away topsoil or scatters seed.
So if you keep your eyes on the wind, you look for the perfect
conditions before sowing, waiting for the wind to die down, or
to blow from the right direction, and so forth.

"When everything goes perfectly—when I have the right
job, when this financial deal goes through, when I have this
amount of money saved—then I'll sow a big offering," you say
if you're looking at the wind.

But I've found out two things about God. First, *He often
asks you to sow when it's not convenient.* Therefore, if you're
always waiting for a convenient time, you may never sow.
And if you never sow, you'll never reap.

Second, *many times God will ask you to sow an amount
that's not convenient.* In fact, if the seed you're planting *is*

convenient or if you know you can afford it, you may be stuck in a comfort zone and you may not be hearing God accurately!

You see, God likes to stretch us out of our comfort zones by asking us to sow more than we were expecting to sow. Remember, He wants us to live by faith, and that takes trust. That's how He desires to take us higher spiritually.

For instance, if you're going through a tough time financially and all you have left in your pocket is a ten dollar bill, the Lord may say to you, "Go ahead and plant that ten dollars. Trust Me."

"Yes, but I might have to miss dinner!" you could argue. You know, it's all right if you go without a little in order to sow. If you wait until all the conditions are favorable, chances are you won't sow. Instead develop a lifestyle of sowing that doesn't depend on the circumstances around you.

Anita and I learned how to apply this principle in our own lives during a time of economic recession. We lived in Canada at the time, and finances were very tight.

However, we continued to sow even when conditions weren't at all favorable in the natural. In fact, when we figured out our tax returns that year, we were amazed to find out we had actually given more than we had earned!

What resulted from our giving during the time it was so inconvenient? We reaped a continual harvest of blessings and finances in the months and years that followed!

There are three reasons why God asks us to give when it's not convenient.

Number one, He wants us to learn how to walk by faith and not by fear. As I said before, He wants us to trust Him enough to step out of our comfort zones and give anyway—convenient or not.

Number two, He wants to use us as those channels of blessing to fulfill someone else's need, and others' needs don't always arise at our convenience. As we allow God to use us as channels, our seed becomes someone else's harvest. And likewise, someone else's seed can be our harvest!

Number three, our giving in obedience, even when it's not convenient, releases the future harvest God knows we will need.

So determine not only to sow but to sow in God's timing. Don't miss the harvest God intends for you by waiting on a surplus or the perfect time to sow, keeping your eyes on the wind! Know that God rewards your faithfulness to sow whether it's convenient or not.

Ask God for Seed

Another guideline to sowing is to ask God for seed! As we read before, **God gives seed to the sower** (2 Corinthians 9:10). You may say, "My problem is that I'm so totally broke, I have nothing to sow." Then ask God for seed, and He'll find a way to get it to you—even if the seed is shirt buttons!

Shirt buttons? As unusual as that sounds, it's exactly what happened years ago to Kenneth Copeland. Today Brother Copeland heads a prospering ministry with about four hundred employees. But more than thirty years ago, he didn't have much of anything—until he suddenly got a revelation of the law of sowing and reaping while sitting in a church service.

As ushers passed the offering plate, Brother Copeland prayed, "Lord, I want to sow into this offering, but I don't have any money. I'm broke! I can't even put food on the table, and my car is falling apart. Help me, Lord. I want to plant, but what am I supposed to do?"

Then Brother Copeland thought about the shirt he was wearing. The only thing he could think of to sow as seed were the buttons on his shirt, so he plucked off a few and dropped them in when the offering plate went by.

God honored his seed of those buttons! Why? Because Brother Copeland gave of his little bit in faith. Now he testifies of the harvest of increase he's reaped again and again from that shirt-button seed simply because he had the heart of a sower!

I'll give you another example. A woman who attended one of my Financial Increase Seminars got a revelation of sowing, but she didn't have any seed. Then the Spirit of God spoke to her spirit, saying, "The seed is in your hand."

Surprised, the woman looked at her hands. She didn't understand. She had no money in her hand, so what was the seed? "Lord, there's nothing in my hand," she said.

The Lord spoke again: "Look again. The seed is in your hand."

So the woman looked at her hands again and said to the Lord, "Oh, You must mean my wedding ring! That's the only thing in my hands." And with a willing heart, she took off her wedding ring and planted it in the offering.

The church didn't know what to do with this woman's seed, so when they gave us the offering, they included her ring in an envelope.

Now this ring wasn't extremely expensive, nor did it have a huge diamond in it. But to this woman, it was the most valuable thing she had, and with the heart of a sower she planted it into God's kingdom.

When my wife saw the wedding ring in the offering, she broke down in tears and prayed, "Lord, I can't take this woman's wedding ring! We'll have to send it back!"

But the Lord told Anita, "Don't you dare refuse that woman's seed! She planted her ring in faith."

A month later, this woman and her husband began trying to purchase a house. When it turned out to cost more than they could afford, the Spirit of God led them to an even bigger house than the one they'd just tried to buy.

The couple couldn't afford the worth of that house either, but when they talked to the owner, he said, "Well, just make me an offer." To make a long story short, they purchased the gorgeous, more expensive home for a third of what it was worth! The woman indeed received a harvest from her wedding-ring seed!

You may wonder what happened to the ring. Anita and I prayed about it, and the Lord told us, "Accept the ring as seed, and a time will come when I will have you plant it back into her life as *your* seed." It was, in fact, seed to us because we could have sold it and used the money.

So this woman doesn't know it yet, but she is getting her ring back! Then she'll have her ring *and* her house—all because she was willing to sow what she had even when it wasn't much.

What I'm saying to you is that before you say, "I don't have any seed," check your wallet, check your bank account, check your closet. Have a garage sale. Or if you know someone who needs a pair of shoes, give him a pair of yours. In fact, give him your best pair!

Don't tell me you don't have any seed, because the Bible says God gives seed to the sower. Now you may not be willing to part with your seed, but you do have *something* you can sow, and God promises to multiply it. And if you even start with a little seed, He'll find a way to get you more.

Get ahold of this truth: When it seems like you don't have anything to sow—even when you don't have a penny to your name—you still possess more than the rest of the world because you have God, and He's the Seed-Giver!

So don't hesitate to ask God for seed. If you're a serious sower, He *will* find a way to get seed into your hand.

Don't Eat Your Seed

Another guideline to sowing is this: God doesn't continue to give seed to a person if that person keeps "eating" the seed. By that I mean the person doesn't rightly value the seed God provides; instead of using it as God intended—for planting— he squanders it on his own wants and needs.

I heard a minister once relate that in the remotest parts of Africa, no matter how bad the climate conditions become— whether typhoons, drought, or extreme heat—you'll never find a native farmer who eats all of his seed.

The farmer knows that one day the weather will change and it will once more be time to plant seed. And when that day comes, if he has eaten his last seed and has nothing to put in the ground, then his chances of survival are over.

Native farmers with no formal education can figure out the basic principle of seedtime and harvest—that seed brings a far greater return in the ground than in our pockets—but how about you and me? It's the same. If we eat the seed God provides for us, we'll not only miss our harvest, we won't have anything left to sow!

For example, suppose my oldest son Aaron comes to me and says, "Dad, I want to start a little business, but I don't have any capital to get it started. If you'll give me the money to begin, I'll work really hard, and the business will explode. Then I'll be able to repay the money you loaned me."

So I say, "Son, I trust you and have faith in you. How much do you want?" Then I write him a check so he can start his business.

But suppose six months later, I find out my son never did start that business. Instead, he just wasted the money on other things. Later, he comes to me again and says, "You know, Dad, I was going to start that business, but something happened and I never got around to doing it. But, listen, I have another, even better idea for a new business. Please just give me the money to get it started. The product will sell like hotcakes!"

So I decide to trust my son once more and give him the money he needs. But again he doesn't do what he promised and instead spends the money.

I guarantee you, the next time my son asks me for money to start a business, I'm more hesitant to give it to him! Well, that's just how the Heavenly Father feels about the person who always eats the seed God gives him.

So if you ever ask the Lord for seed and He faithfully provides it for you, make sure you faithfully sow it.

Any seed not sown is seed not grown.

Live Off Your Giving

Let me share another guideline for sowing: Live off your giving. Don't live off your seed; plant it and live off your harvest.

I'll tell you what I mean. One of the most obvious ways God provides seed for you to sow is through your job. The Bible says:

Let the thief steal no more, but rather let him be industrious, making an honest living with his own hands, SO THAT HE MAY BE ABLE TO GIVE TO THOSE IN NEED.

—Ephesians 4:28

The principle in this verse doesn't just apply to former thieves; it applies to all of us.

Why should we get jobs—just so we can fill up a bank account? No, that's not what this Scripture says. It says to make an honest living *so we can give.*

You see, God wants you involved in the cycle of seedtime and harvest. Therefore, He'll help you find a good job to provide you with seed to sow.

I know many Christians who live a quality of life far above their paycheck. They can do that because they've tapped into God's law of seedtime and harvest by making the decision, "My paycheck's going to be a source of seed for sowing, and I'm going to live off my harvest!"

But too many Christians make the mistake of paying their bills with their paycheck and leaving nothing to plant into God's kingdom. And yet they wonder why they're always broke!

If you were a farmer and God gave you a bag of seed, what would He say if you promptly cooked all the seed and ate it? He'd tell you, "I gave you this seed to *plant,* not to eat!" You're not to live off the seed!"

In the same way, your job is your seedbag, not your source of security. Therefore, you must let your *giving*—not your paycheck—produce your living. Step over into heaven's economy, where there are no "black Mondays," no roller-coaster interest rates, no fluctuating values on the currency. In heaven, the economy is always good, and the supply is always never-ending.

So remember, you're working for seed to sow toward your harvest!

Sow Bountifully, Reap Bountifully

We find an additional guideline for sowing in Second Corinthians 9:6 (NKJV): **"He who sows sparingly will also reap sparingly, and he who sows bountifully will also reap bountifully."** This verse proves that God doesn't determine our harvest; we do!

Do you want to experience great prosperity in your life? Then large harvests require large amounts of seed, because the more you sow, the more you reap.

A farmer determines the size of his harvest initially at seedtime. If he wants ten acres of crops harvested, then he plants seed in ten acres of ground. There's no other way.

So how much should you give? Give as much as you possibly can. Remember, *you* determine your own harvest!

Give Cheerfully

Verse 7 goes on to say, **"So let each one give as he purposes in his heart, not grudgingly or of necessity; for God loves a cheerful giver."** You see, God doesn't want you to give under compulsion. If you're giving only because you feel like you have to, then you're not giving in faith and you're not fully convinced that the law of sowing and reaping works.

Notice what kind of giver God likes—a *cheerful* one! *The Amplified Bible* renders verse 7 this way: **"Let each one [give] as he has made up his own mind and purposed in his heart, not reluctantly or sorrowfully or under compulsion, for God loves (that is, He takes pleasure in, prizes above other things, and is unwilling to abandon or to do without) a cheerful (joyous, prompt-to-do-it) giver—whose heart is in his giving."**

God takes pleasure in a joyous, prompt-to-do-it giver! Why? Because a cheerful giver gives by faith, and faith is the very thing that pleases God (Hebrews 11:6).

I'm more excited about giving to God than I am about anything else. For instance, I used to own a big company, and when checks would come in the mail, my staff members and I didn't waste a minute of time—as soon as the checks were out of the envelopes, we calculated our tithes and offerings.

Then I could hardly wait for the church doors to open so I could bring my tithes and offerings into God's storehouse. I wanted to be a prompt-to-do-it giver—and I still do!

Verse 7 emphasizes that God "prizes above other things" a cheerful giver. When I read that phrase, I thought of hunters who display their greatest hunting trophy—the head of a moose, bear, or bull elk—above their mantelpiece. And whenever a visitor comes to the house, that hunter says, "Hey, come over to the mantelpiece. I want to show you the trophy I prize above all of my others."

Something similar must take place up in heaven. God says, "Hey, angels, come here and let Me show you something. You see that believer down there? I prize that one! He's My trophy."

"Why is that believer Your trophy, Lord?" the angels ask.

God answers, "Look at the attitude in which he gives. He's such a cheerful, prompt giver! Every time I even whisper to him to give, he writes a check without hesitation. Every time I bless him with something, he asks me, 'Who is this for, Lord?' I'm unwilling to do without that one because he's a faithful channel. Now just watch as I release his harvest!"

You see, God loves a cheerful giver!

Give as You Purpose in Your Heart

Notice something else Second Corinthians 9:7 says: **"So let each one give AS HE PURPOSES IN HIS HEART...."** In other words, let God speak to your heart about how much to give.

God is omnipresent. He knows your future; He's been there already, and He knows what your needs will be before you do. But He also knows the financial obstacles the enemy will try to put in your way.

So if you always give what you think is a good figure without ever checking your heart, your amount may not match what God wants you to give. He may prompt you to sow a certain amount because He sees a future need in your life that will require the very harvest you could sow toward *if* you listened to your heart. Therefore, purpose to give the amount God lays on your heart.

And here's something else to consider when planting seed. Suppose God leads you to give a needy person some money and that person uses the money for the wrong thing, such as drugs or alcohol. Or suppose the Lord leads you to sow a large offering into a church and later that church mismanages its funds and falls apart. Do the wrong actions of a person or church you've blessed cancel out your harvest?

No! The law of sowing and reaping still works for you because you obeyed God's leading and gave as you purposed in your heart. Now He may hold that person or church accountable for misusing the money, but God nonetheless rewards your obedience to sow. And the harvest remains yours to claim.

Here's the bottom line: The Spirit of the living God lives in your heart, He speaks to you there, and He tells your heart what to do. What it means to give as you purpose in your heart is that the moment an offering is announced, you check your heart and ask, "Lord, what do You want me to give?" And you give the amount He leads you to give, knowing He will bless your seed no matter how the church manages it.

Don't be moved by circumstances—by the bills and such that surround you. Be moved by one thing only: the Spirit of God speaking to your heart.

God's Definition of Prosperity

What happens when you sow bountifully and cheerfully as you purpose in your heart to give? You get yourself in position to enjoy *God's* definition of prosperity, which is described in 2 Corinthians 9:8. In other words, as you fulfill verses 6 and 7, you get to verse 8! **"And God is able to make all grace (every favor and earthly blessing) come to you in abundance, so that you may always and under all circumstances and whatever the need be self-sufficient [possessing enough to require no aid or support and furnished in abundance for every good work and charitable donation]."**

Now *that is* prosperity according to the God of too much! Essentially, this verse tells us we should never have a need in our lives which God isn't in the process of meeting.

God's definition of prosperity is this: "I will give you enough to meet every single one of your needs." But He doesn't stop there; because He realizes we need to be flowing rivers, not clogged-up dams. God also says, "Not only will I meet all your needs, but I will give you enough excess to give into *every* good work."

That means if your heart is drawn to ten good works, you'll have enough to give freely to all ten works. If you know of twenty-five good works, you'll be able to give to all twenty-five—in great abundance, with great joy!

Unfortunately, for the most part, Christians have not reached that level of supernatural prosperity yet. But it will start to happen as we change the way we think, seeing things the way God sees them.

So let me stir up your imagination a little so you can picture yourself living according to God's definition of prosperity.

Suppose your church starts an evangelism program to reach out to people in your city and it's going to cost five thousand dollars to implement it. Getting people saved is a good work, so you write a check for seven thousand dollars and send it to the pastor.

The pastor says, "Thank you, but we only needed five thousand dollars."

You reply, "Oh, no, it's all right. Use the rest for any unanticipated expenses. Otherwise, apply the extra funds to your next project." That's giving in abundance to a good work!

Or imagine yourself in this situation. The pastor says, "We want to get this church building paid off."

You ask, "Well, how much do you need?"

"Oh, about a hundred thousand dollars."

"Okay, I'll write you a check for the total amount."

How about this scenario: The pastor tells you, "One of our missionaries is returning from Africa in order to travel from church to church, trying to raise enough money to buy a badly needed school bus."

You say, "No, no, Pastor, tell the missionary to stay in Africa! How much is the bus?"

"Forty thousand dollars."

"Okay, I'll write you a check to cover the cost. That missionary doesn't need to spend so much time and energy looking for money. I want to give to every good work!"

Those are just a few examples of living according to God's definition of prosperity. Are we there yet? Maybe not, but those of us who take God at His Word will be!

It's unfortunate that only the unsaved seem to stand up and state publicly that they're giving a billion dollars away— if anyone is going to give away a billion dollars, it ought to be the children of God, giving to every good work of the kingdom!

Cause Others To Glorify God Through Your Giving

When we're living according to the level of God's definition of prosperity, the following principle becomes an inevitable result:

Thus you will be ENRICHED IN ALL THINGS AND IN EVERY WAY, so that you can be generous,

and [your generosity as it is] administered by us will bring forth thanksgiving to God.
—2 Corinthians 9:11

Why will we be enriched in all things? Because we sow seed cheerfully. To us, giving isn't a chore—it's a joy!

And every time we give freely and joyfully from our hearts, we bring forth thanksgiving unto God according to verse 11. You see, the person who receives the blessing says, "Thank You, Lord!"

I want to be someone who continually causes people to thank God for His goodness!

You certainly are not going to cause people to glorify God if you're a stingy Christian. But when you give freely, the way God does, people see Jesus in you and thank the Lord for His love as it is reflected through your life!

Make Heavenly *Deposits* Before Making *Withdrawals*

Philippians 4 gives another important guideline to sowing. Let's start with the familiar verse 19, which many Christians use to claim prosperity: **"But my God shall supply all your need according to his riches in glory by Christ Jesus"** (KJV).

People read that and say, "Hallelujah! God will supply all of my needs!" That's true, but do you know what I found out out? I found that you can't get to Philippians 4:19 without going through the door of Philippians 4:15.

You see, Scripture must be read in context to know who is talking and to whom. We can't just pull out a Scripture and say, "Paul said it, so my God *shall* supply all my needs!"

So to find out who can stand on the promise in verse 19, we have to start in verse 15. Paul is writing to the church in Philippi, to believers like you and me.

And you Philippians yourselves well know that in the early days of the Gospel ministry, when I left Macedonia, no church (assembly) entered into partnership with me and opened up [a debit and credit] account in giving and receiving except you only.

—Philippians 4:15

Paul was so busy doing God's work—traveling, teaching, preaching, and starting churches—that he needed people to support him. Philippi, the poorest church Paul had established, nonetheless, chose to partner with him.

During a twenty-year relationship with Paul, the people had been serious sowers, giving into God's work as a congregation.

So Paul wrote, "No church entered into partnership with me and opened up a credit and debit account except you." Notice this account was opened for two reasons: for *giving* and for *receiving*.

In essence, Paul meant, "Philippians, you and I are partners. Your giving into the work of God has opened for you an account in heaven for both debit and credit. Now you can not only partake in giving, but in receiving as well."

The heavenly account is both a debit *and* credit account. That's an important point. Can you imagine, for example, someone walking into a bank where he doesn't have an account and saying to the bank teller, "I want to make a withdrawal"?

The teller would say, "You've never made a deposit—in fact, you don't even have an account here! You have the nerve to come into this bank and ask for money? Are you crazy?"

Unfortunately, that's what too many Christians do with God. They pray, "God, give me money! I need to make my mortgage payment and my car payment."

God asks, "Have you opened an account in heaven and made any deposits here?"

"Uh, well, let's see—oh, yes! Three years ago I gave two dollars in the offering."

You see, people expect to make withdrawals from heaven; they just don't want to make any deposits. But you can't withdraw a harvest of blessings from your "account" unless you have planted seeds toward it first. Your giving *creates* your harvest.

In the natural, when you open an account in a bank and deposit money into it, you obtain the legal right to stand at the counter and say to the teller, "I want to make a withdrawal."

Paul tried to get the same idea across to the Philippians. They had become partners with Paul through their giving, which opened an account in heaven—where credit is multiplied. Therefore, Paul said, the Philippians had every legal right to make a withdrawal; they had sowed to their heavenly account, so they could expect a harvest from it.

The same principle holds true with you. When you give into God's kingdom as a lifestyle sower, you open a heavenly account. Every time you give, you make a deposit into that account, which means you have a scriptural right to stand in faith and make a withdrawal on your account in heaven for what you need.

Some believers just don't understand that. They write out a hundred-dollar check, and as they put it in the offering plate, they say, "Bye, bye, one hundred dollars!"

What do those believers mean by that? They obviously don't know that with their offering they're opening up a heavenly account, an investment into God's kingdom with a guaranteed return!

For example, if you deposited a hundred-dollar check into your savings account, would you say as you gave it to the teller, "Bye, bye, one hundred dollars"? No, that would be silly.

You know where that money is going—into your account. You know you're going to earn interest on that one hundred dollars and that at any time you can come back and withdraw it because the account is in your name.

Have as much faith in your heavenly account as you do in your earthly bank account!

There's a great difference, however, between depositing money in your heavenly account and depositing it in your earthly account. *The difference is in the return.* God doesn't promise just a six or seven-percent return, as a bank does. He promises a thirty, sixty, and hundredfold return. In fact, He even goes beyond that; His return far surpasses what you could ask, think, dream, or imagine (Ephesians 3:20)!

I once read an interview in the *Financial Post* of the chairman of a very successful financial company. The chairman, a Christian, is known as an investment guru.

In the article, the interviewer asked, "Given your phenomenal success in the realm of investment, what would your advice be to the layman looking for the best place to invest his money?"

Guess what the expert for the *Financial Post* said? "Invest in God," he advised. "You'll receive the greatest return you've ever experienced. The reason I'm so financially successful is that I give liberally for the cause of the Gospel."

That man was absolutely right. No bank, retirement fund, term deposit, or mutual fund can guarantee you a better return than investing in the Gospel. When you truly understand that fact, you will *run* to make heavenly deposits in your debit and credit account with God!

Store Up Treasures in Heaven

Scripture gives us more insight about our heavenly bank account:

> **Do not gather and heap up and store up for yourselves treasures on earth, where moth and rust and worm consume and destroy, and where thieves break through and steal.**
> **But gather and heap up and store for yourselves treasures in heaven, where neither moth nor rust nor worm consume and destroy, and where thieves do not break through and steal.**
> —Matthew 6:19,20

These Scriptures couldn't be talking about spiritual treasures, simply because we can't store spiritual treasures on earth. No, Jesus is talking about material treasures, saying, "If you store those treasures on earth, they are subject to the world's uncertain economy. But if you store them in heaven, they are subject to heaven's absolute principles of increase."

You see, some of the richest people I know live in fear of losing their wealth or being kidnapped and ransomed. They set twenty security alarms all over their house, trying to keep thieves from stealing their riches.

Why do these people fear losing their riches? They're afraid because the treasures they've stored up on earth belong to this world system and therefore are subject to loss and destruction.

So how do we store up treasures in heaven? We know we don't literally send our material goods and riches to heaven to enjoy them in our mansions for eternity. We won't need riches in heaven! The streets there are paved with gold, and the gates are of pearl. Why would we need money in heaven?

These Scriptures are talking about making heavenly deposits for earthly withdrawals and trusting in heaven's economy instead of the world's economy—about sowing instead of hoarding.

Every time you give into God's kingdom, moth, rust, time, and changing economies cannot destroy you're investment. You sow into heaven's economy expecting to see a return of wealth manifested on the earth.

Matthew 6:21 (KJV) says, **"For where your treasure is, there will your heart be also"**. Think about that. You can tell where a person stands with the Lord by what he does with his money. Where he puts treasure, (on earth or in heaven) reveals where his heart is.

So the more treasure you store up in your heavenly bank account by your giving, the more you prove how much you are trusting, relying, leaning on, and believing in God. Do you think God likes that? Yes! And the truth is, it's impossible for us to please Him any other way!

Let's go back to our text. Paul had a lot to say to the Philippians about storing up riches in heaven:

> **For even in Thessalonica you sent [me contributions] for my needs, not only once but a second time.**
> **Not that I seek or am eager for [your] gift, but I do seek and am eager for the fruit which increases to your credit—the harvest of blessing that is accumulating to your account.**
> —Philippians 4:16,17

Notice Paul says that fruit *increases*. This is another reference to the awesome power within a seed to multiply. The Philippians' harvest accumulated in their account by the multiplication of the seed they sowed into the work of God. You see, when you store up riches in heaven, blessings *accumulate* in your heavenly account!

Your Giving Comes Before God's Throne

Did you know that God actually watches as you store up treasures in your heavenly account? It's true. In fact, your giving comes before His throne.

God is very aware of our giving. Verse 18 says, **"...the gifts you sent me...are the fragrant odor of an offering and sacrifice which God welcomes and in which He delights."**

The Bible also reflects this same truth in the account of Cornelius, a Roman centurion. Cornelius was **"a devout man who venerated God and treated Him with reverential obedience, as did all his household; and he GAVE MUCH ALMS to the people and PRAYED CONTINUALLY to God"** (Acts 10:2).

One day Cornelius had a visitation from an angel, who said to him: **"Your prayers and your [generous] gifts to**

the poor have come up [as a sacrifice] to God and have been remembered by him" (v. 4).

Now we don't know much about Cornelius, but two things we do know: He was a man of prayer and a giver. That's why the angel told him, "Your prayers *and* your giving have come before the throne room of God."

Every time you pray according to the scriptures, your prayers come before the throne of God. God hears your prayers and wants to answer them. But God also sees every time you give, and He's just as interested in your giving as He is your praying! He knows whether or not you're a sower, because He literally has an account of your giving.

Every time you give, it's a fragrant odor to God. God gets excited when you give—it delights Him! Why? He takes pleasure in seeing His children prosper, and they only prosper when they live the lifestyle of a sower!

Visualize something like this in heaven: A group of Christians accumulate tall stacks of prayers in God's throne room—prayers that have ascended to Him from their hearts over the years. But these same people's stacks of giving, (which also ascend to God's throne throughout their lives), are so small they're hard to locate.

Those Christians arrive in heaven and ask God, "Lord, why did I always struggle financially during my earthly life?" God will say, "Come over here, Child; I want to show you something. See that huge pile over there? Those were your prayers. But do you see that little ant mound in the corner? That was your giving!"

Therefore, as we learn God's guidelines for sowing, we realize that He sees our giving and is pleased with us for it.

The Divine Promise of Abundant Supply

Let's say you've followed the example of the Philippian church. You have opened up an account in heaven and you make deposits by sowing into the kingdom. You lay up your treasures in heaven, and you please God by your sowing.

Having fulfilled the conditions of faithful giving (vv. 15-18), you now have a legal right to stand in faith on the promise in verse 19: **"But my God shall supply all your need according to his riches in glory by Christ Jesus"** (KJV).

The actuality of this incredible promise rests on the balance of the account you open in heaven. You determine that balance by your sowing.

But notice the verse starts out, **"My God shall supply...."** Who are we talking about here? He's the Creator of heaven and earth, and the sun, moon, and stars. He's the One who knit you in your mother's womb and knew you before the foundations of the earth. *He* is the God who will supply all of your needs!

Then it continues, "My God *shall* supply...." It *does not* say, "My God *may* supply if He's in a good mood on that particular day"—no, He *shall* supply. That word *shall* is a strong, affirmative word. And why shall God supply all my needs? He will because I'm a sower! I have a covenant agreement with the God of the universe, and as I keep my part of the bargain, He promises to keep His part.

Notice also that verse 19 doesn't say, "Social Security shall supply," or "My job shall supply." No, it's "My *God* shall supply."

"But you don't understand," you might insist, "I just got laid off my job!" But you see, your job was never your supply. God is your Supply, and He's never gone out of business yet!

Next, it says, "My God shall supply all of my needs." What does *all* mean? It means all! It means God shall supply all of your spiritual needs, emotional needs, physical needs, and financial needs—all your needs according to what? According to your education? According to your job? No, *according to His riches in glory by Christ Jesus!*

In other words, God supplies your needs based on what Jesus already did when He redeemed you from the curse of poverty. Jesus already took care of your supply, so just be faithful to deposit into your heavenly account in order to have something to draw from.

He will supply our needs according to *His riches!* That's quite a promise.

You see, we're in partnership with our Father, who is in real estate—He owns the universe! Oh, yes, and let me remind you, our Dad also has a cattle business. In fact, He owns the cattle on a thousand hills (Psalm 50:10)! And He's into precious stones too—all the diamond and gold mines of the earth belong to Him (Psalm 50:12; Haggai 2:8)!

Needless to say, our Father is *wealthy*. And it's according to *His* riches *in glory* that our needs will be supplied!

Have you ever seen the prince or princess of a kingdom driving around in a twenty-year-old, beat-up, two-toned (and the second color is rust) Volkswagen? No way. Something would be wrong with that picture, because it doesn't reflect the earthly glory that befits royalty.

The same thing applies to you, because you're the King's kid! "Do you mean God wants me to have a nice car?" you ask. Yes! "And He wants me to have a nice home?" Yes! In fact, God wants you to have the best of everything.

Christians ought to be the best-dressed people on earth. They ought to drive nice cars. After all, they are ambassadors of Christ, and they represent Him.

If you were an ambassador for your country to another nation, the foreign nation's perception of your country would be based largely on its perception of you and your lifestyle.

Similarly, in your role as an ambassador for Christ, if you are broke and can barely make ends meet, your financial condition doesn't accurately represent or glorify God. People will say, "I sure don't want to be a part of the kingdom you represent!"

God's kingdom is one of everlasting supply. We can rightly represent Him on the earth because we don't base our supply on interest rates or recessions—there is no recession in heaven—but on our sowing to a heavenly account.

Recognize who your Supplier is. Believe in His faithfulness to supply what you need just as Daniel did when he was thrown into the lions' den. Daniel slept among hungry lions all night without being eaten because he understood God's utter faithfulness to supply His need for protection and deliverance!

When you truly understand the faithfulness of your Heavenly Father to supply whatever you need, it will set you free from poverty and lack for the rest of your life. As you follow God's specific guidelines for sowing into His kingdom, God absolutely guarantees that financial blessings will chase you down *according to His riches in glory*!

Chapter 10
Three Principles of Seedtime and Harvest

"Be not deceived; God is not mocked: for WHAT-SOEVER A MAN SOWETH, THAT SHALL HE ALSO REAP."

—Galatians 6:7 KJV

Sowing precedes reaping. Seedtime precedes harvest. These simple truths are laws which God has placed on the earth. As long as this planet exists, that law is going to stay in place: "While the earth remaineth, SEEDTIME AND HARVEST, and cold and heat, and summer and winter, and day and night SHALL NOT CEASE" (Genesis 8:22 KJV).

While this earth remains, we will experience day and night, winter and summer, heat and cold. Does day still follow night? Yes. Does summer still follow winter? Yes. Do cold and heat still exist? Yes. Then it logically follows that the law of seedtime and harvest remain in effect on this earth.

Within the law of seedtime and harvest, three primary principles operate: you always reap what you sow, you will always reap more than you sow, and you always reap in a different season.

Principle Number 1: You Always Reap What You Sow

Notice that Genesis 8:22 doesn't say, "harvest and seed-time" because harvest never comes first. We've already learned that the common belief "Get, and then you can give" is opposite to the way God thinks. It's just not God's correct order for doing things. You sow before you reap.

So let's look at the first law of seedtime and harvest: *You will always reap what you sow.* We can see when God first set this law into motion on the earth:

And God said, Let the earth put forth [tender] vegetation: plants yielding seed and fruit trees yielding fruit whose seed is in itself, EACH ACCORDING TO ITS KIND, upon the earth. And it was so.
—Genesis 1:11

Every seed reproduces after its own kind. So if you plant tomato seeds, don't wait for corn to come up—it's not going to happen!

Now this law can work for both good and bad. If you sow good seed, such as kindness and love, you will reap a harvest of kindness and love in your life. But if you sow bad seed, such as strife and bitterness, you're in a world of trouble—a multiplied harvest of strife and bitterness is on its way back to you!

Galatians 6:7 states the law of seedtime and harvest in a different way: **"Be not deceived; God is not mocked: FOR WHATSOEVER A MAN SOWETH, THAT SHALL HE ALSO REAP"** (KJV).

Paul wrote to believers, saying, "Don't be deceived; God is not mocked."

I read that Scripture many times but it still took me awhile to understand it. I thought, *Let's get serious. If you're going to mock anyone, you pick on someone your own size, and for goodness' sake, you don't pick on the Creator of heaven and earth. He's bigger than you are, and anyway, where could you go and how far could you run to get away from Him?*

So I talked to God about it. I said, "Lord, what Christian in his right mind would mock You? Not one Christian I know who actually loves You would start mocking You."

He replied, "Christians mock Me daily without knowing it by violating the law of seedtime and harvest. They are deceived."

"How are they deceived, Lord?"

"They actually sow bad seed and expect a good harvest!"

I thought about that and realized how true it is. Sometimes Christians rationalize planting bad seed. They say of their company's product, "Well, I'll just cut back on the quality this time until I'm over this financial hump." Or they'll say, "I won't keep my word in this situation because it would be to my own detriment." Or maybe they rationalize, "I promised to pay my creditors that bill in thirty days, but I think I'll take six months instead—it's better for my budget."

After planting bad seed, people often think they've gotten away with it just because they don't reap any immediate negative consequence. But that harvest hasn't been canceled; it just takes awhile for seed to grow. At some point down the road, they *will* reap from the bad seed they have sown.

Then those same people cry out, "Why are these bad things happening to me?" But all they need to do is look back over the past months and years and see what kind of seeds they've been planting. Oftentimes, they're reaping a harvest of bad seeds they've sown.

The repercussions of sowing bad seed is like the process of erosion. When you sit by a river and watch it flow, you're not able to immediately see the erosion that's in progress. You would have to observe the riverbank for a period of time to actually see the effects of erosion on the land. But whether you see it happen before your eyes or not, erosion nonetheless takes place as you sit on the riverbank.

So don't be deceived; you can't mock God by thinking whatever you sow you won't reap. That law is working in your life whether you know it or not, and you are reaping today what you sowed in the past.

'The Devil Did It!'

Notice Galatians 6:7 doesn't say, "Whatsoever *Satan* sows, that will you reap." No, it says whatsoever *you* sow, you will also reap.

Many times when bad things happen in our lives, we say, "Look what the devil is doing to me!" While it's true that the devil does sometimes attack us, if we would look back three months, six months, or even several years, we might find that in some situations we are actually reaping the harvest of seed we've sown ourselves.

For instance, someone might pray, "Help me get out of debt, God!"

"How did you get in debt in the first place, Child?" He would respond.

"Well, you know, it was those credit cards. They made it so easy to go into the store and just buy whatever I wanted."

But a person who charges more than he can afford on his credit cards actually sows seeds of debt, which he reaps as a multiplied harvest of debt as high interest rates steadily increase the amount he owes.

Of course, we have all made silly mistakes at one time or another for which we have reaped the consequences. I know I certainly have.

For example, one time God spoke through my wife concerning a business deal in which I wanted to invest fifty thousand dollars. Anita had a clear check in her heart that indicated I wasn't supposed to invest in this deal, and by that God was telling us, "Don't do it."

But I told Anita, "Honey, this is a one-in-a-million kind of deal! We're going to make so much money from this. I *have* to go for it!"

So I did. And guess how much I lost? Everything I invested.

Now I could have said, "Oh, look what the devil did to me through this business deal," but no, I couldn't blame the devil. I made a wrong decision without listening to what God had to say about it. Had I listened to God first, I would have heard what He was trying to tell me—that it was a wrong move. But instead, I planted bad seed and then reaped a harvest after the same kind.

We will always reap the harvest of seed we plant. If you say, "I want to be treated well," what kind of seed are you planting? Have you treated others with kindness? Or maybe you say, "I want people to smile at me." Then take the frown off *your* face! "I want people to give to me," you complain. But what have *you* been giving?

Seedtime and harvest is a *law*, which governs the entire universe. You can't escape it just because you don't believe it works. Whether you believe in sowing and reaping or not, you *will* reap whatever kind of seeds you sow in life. So as you sow, make sure you sow *good* seeds. In fact, make sure you sow your best!

Sow Your Best

As a sower, constantly look for ways to sow into the kingdom—and it doesn't just have to be money. You can sow a pair of shoes, a jacket, a tie, even your time and energy. The truth is, anything you possess can become seed to sow.

But make sure you ask yourself, *What do I want to reap?* If you'll ask yourself that question before you sow, you're likely to give your best and not your worst.

For example, what if someone said, "Honey, the church needs a television, and we have that set in the basement that hasn't worked in three years. Why don't we give it to the church?" Be careful. You may end up reaping a harvest of broken-down goods yourself!

Remember, whatever you sow comes back to you. Every seed reproduces after its own kind. So if you want to reap junk, start sowing junk.

I know someone who constantly takes her best clothes out of her closet and gives them away. She told me, "I do that for two reasons. First, if I give my best, that's what I'll reap. And second, I'm cleaning out my closet because when I reap my harvest, I'll need closet space!"

Now of course, you need to stay balanced about what you give away. In other words, follow God's leading in order to know how much and to whom you should sow.

"But God never speaks to me about giving," you say. If that's what you think, I challenge you to ask, "Lord, is there anyone You want me to give something to?"

If you will quiet your heart and listen, it won't take long before you sense the Holy Spirit's leading to sow your best into someone's life. Why is that? Because God knows that as you sow your best, He can prepare *His* best as your harvest!

We Reap What We Sow: Personal Testimonies

As a teenager, my wife Anita had a friend who was so poor, she couldn't afford to buy new shoes. Anita's friend wore shoes with holes in them, and every time it rained, the girl's feet would get wet.

Anita, who had been a Christian since she was seven, prayed, "Lord, why don't You do something about my friend's shoes?"

The Lord responded, "Why don't *you* do something about it?"

"I can't do anything, Lord," Anita said. "I only have two pairs of shoes—a nice pair that I really like and another, older pair that are so tight on me, they make my heels bleed." But then she thought about it and said, "Well, I guess I could give her those older, too-small shoes."

But the Lord gently reminded her, "Daughter, are you ready to reap what you sow?"

"Oh," Anita said. "I guess I better give her my good shoes then."

So the next day Anita gave her friend the favorite pair of shoes, and Anita wore the shoes that hurt her feet and made her heels bleed.

But this story doesn't end on a "poor Anita" note. Today Anita has two closets full of shoes of every conceivable style and color! Why does she? Because she's been a sower all her life and she sowed her best shoes into a friend's life, that seed has reproduced and multiplied after its own kind!

Anita and I have also experienced this law in operation in our lives together. When we were first married, we actually became millionaires through a very successful business venture.

But approximately one year later, we suddenly lost all our money, our cars, and our home through a series of events. (What really happened is that we lacked the wisdom of God to not only make but *keep* our first million—but we're not going to make that same mistake again!)

I remember how devastated I felt as I drove away from the home we'd lost. After we lost everything, every one of our possessions fit inside a small, borrowed truck.

For a year, we struggled through a very tough time. I couldn't find any work, and we had no money, no home, and no vehicle of our own. Finally, we ended up staying in my father-in-law's house.

But during the following months when we were completely broke, we never ran out of food. Food found its way to our home all the time! You see, back when we'd had money, we continually fed other people, taking them out for dinner, sending them food, cooking them meals, and such. We constantly gave, gave, gave. So when we needed food, food was supplied in abundance!

If you're always giving food, you'll always have food supplied when you need it. How do I know that? I know it because seedtime and harvest is a law set in motion by God, and it's just as real as, the law of gravity.

By the way, throughout that very rough year of trials, we maintained the joy of the Lord, never giving up on God! At times, the only money we had was one dollar. But instead of spending it on our needs, we'd sow it. Do you know what we found out through that experience? The God of multiplication can do much more with a dollar than we can!

During that year we also never went without a car, although we no longer owned one ourselves. Someone would show up with a vehicle and say, "You can drive this for the next two months." After those two months, someone else would show up with another one. And they always brought the cars to us filled with gas!

Today my wife and I own three cars, two of which were given to us. I never wondered why cars have always been supplied to us when we needed them, because in the past, we sowed several cars into other people's lives, giving them away to those who needed them. And every seed reproduces after its own kind!

I'm convinced God provided for us throughout that difficult time because we had been serious sowers. And even when the bottom fell out of our finances, we never stopped sowing; therefore, we've always reaped.

And it wasn't long before God brought us out of that financial trial—*completely* out. Since then God's blessed us abundantly in every area of our lives!

Sow in the Area of Your Need

What do *you* need today? Take advantage of this first principle of seedtime and harvest—that you always reap what you sow—and sow in the area of your need. Do you need your debts canceled? Plant seeds into your church to help get *its* debt canceled. Do you need more clothes? Then give away some of your nice clothes to someone who needs them more than you do.

I have sowed many items of clothing myself. For instance, I've given away many ties, and over the years, I've reaped many ties. I remember one day as I was ushering at church, I greeted a man and helped him find a seat.

As I seated him, I told him, "That's a wonderful tie you're wearing. God has blessed you!"

"Oh, thank you," the man said, "I just bought it at the mall. It's brand new!"

After the service, he came over to me and said, "I have to repent."

"Why?" I asked.

"The Lord told me to give you this tie the moment I met you, and I didn't do it. But here it is now," and he handed me the tie. I was surprised, but I realized that it was a manifestation of my "tie harvest"!

Another time someone else walked over to me in church and gave me an expensive suit jacket that fit me perfectly.

Each time something like this has happened to me, I recognize that I am reaping from the harvest of seeds I've planted for clothing. Meanwhile, I just keep on sowing!

Now maybe you don't need clothes, but you don't want to deal with car payments anymore. Then find someone who needs help making a car payment, and pay it for him! When you start planting car payments, then a harvest of car payments will show up!

Or you could say, "I'm believing God for a house." So help someone pay a monthly mortgage payment. You see, as you do, you're planting seed for your own house! I'm telling you, this principle works in every area, both good and bad.

And if what you need is money, then find a way to sow money into good ground. Maybe you could sell all those items stored away in the garage that you know you'll never use again.

So many of us are "keepers of stuff." We hang on to stuff, thinking, *"You never know when you might need it!"* But that day never comes, so we continually gather more stuff to pile on top of the old stuff. Then finally, we need a garage sale to get rid of it all!

Well, why not sell all that accumulated stuff you don't need? And then use the money you make as seed to plant for your own harvest of finances!

So ransack your cupboards with the determination, "I *have* to find something to give!" Tap into the principle of reaping what you've sown. Somewhere in your house waits seed that could be someone else's harvest. And the moment you find it and sow it, you release your own harvest of blessing!

Principle Number 2: You Always Reap More Than You Sow

Jesus related a parable about a sower who planted seed into four kinds of ground. His description in Matthew 13:8 of good ground reveals the second principle of seedtime and harvest: *You always reap more than you sow.* **"Other seeds fell on good soil, and yielded grain—some a hundred times as much as was sown, some sixty times as much, and some thirty."**

Only seed planted in good ground can reproduce with such force.

Sow Only in Good Ground

How do you identify good ground for sowing? First of all, be led by the Holy Spirit. As you are sensitive to His voice, He'll direct you to good ground.

Second, look for ground that already bears fruit for God's kingdom.

For example, some organizations say, "Send us money to feed the hungry in such-and-such country." Then you find out later that they spent ninety cents of every dollar on administrative costs and that only ten cents of each dollar actually fed the hungry! That's *not* good ground!

So be careful where you sow. Make sure you find good ground.

A ministry that's good ground is a ministry where God's Word is fully taught and people are getting saved, healed, delivered, and set free. Ministers who believe in seedtime and harvest and are big givers themselves are good ground.

On the other hand, if a ministry asks for your help because it's about to go under, chances are it's not good ground. Do you know why ministries often go under? Usually, it's from not giving. If a ministry were to practice planting seed, that ministry would also reap a harvest.

So when I'm looking for good ground in which to sow, one of the first things I want to know about a ministry is this: Does that ministry believe in sowing? Because if a ministry isn't planting seed, its harvest will eventually dry up. It becomes stony ground instead of good ground. One day their supporters might receive one of those letters from them that says, "Going out of business."

Give, and It Shall Be Given

Jesus Himself stated a powerful Scripture about the second principle of seedtime and harvest—that you always reap more than you sow:

> **Give, and it shall be given unto you; good measure, pressed down, and shaken together, and running over, shall men give into your bosom. For with the same measure that ye mete withal** [or deal out] **it shall be measured to you again.**
>
> —Luke 6:38 KJV

This Scripture affirms, "Give, and it *shall* be given unto you"—not "it *may* be given unto you." In other words, you can count on it. If you sow, it shall come back to you as harvest.

But notice God doesn't give the harvest back in the same form as you gave the seed. When it's time for harvest, God gives it back *pressed down*.

What does that mean? Well, think of a can of concentrated orange juice. It starts out in a "pressed down" form that fits into a small can. But in its final form with water added, the orange juice fills an entire pitcher. In a similar way, our harvest comes back to us in concentrated form, ready to expand and encompass our entire lives!

Also, the harvest comes back into our lives *shaken together and running over*. If you want a picture of what that means, just shake a can of pop and then open it! That's how we're supposed to receive our harvest: in a bubbling-over measure greater than we sowed.

Remember, we serve the first Giver, who gave His only begotten Son so He could receive back many sons and daughters. God knows how this law of multiplication works, because He's the One who set it in place!

Finally, this Scripture promises that after we've given, men will give back to us "into our bosom." The wealth needed for the body of Christ to take the Gospel around the world already exists on this planet, but believers are just waiting for men to pour that wealth into their bosom.

More Christians don't see this promise manifested in their lives because they try to reverse the sequence of events, saying, "When I receive increase that is pressed down, shaken together, and running over as men pour money into my bosom, *then* I will give." No, we've already seen that it doesn't work that way. Giving comes first. It's really simple—no sowing equals no harvest.

One day I was meditating on this Scripture, and I prayed, "Lord, I'm so excited about this promise. I'm a giver, and I'm expecting my harvest to be given back to me, pressed down, shaken together, and running over shall men pour into my bosom. So which man are You going to use, Lord?"

The Lord replied, "It may be the one you never expected, so don't worry about trying to figure it out."

"Well, when is it going to happen, Lord? When will men start pouring into my bosom?"

Instead of answering my question, the Lord said, "You know, Nasir, you're one of those men."

"What do You mean?"

"I mean, whose bosom have *you* been pouring into lately?"

So there I was, faced with that seedtime-and-harvest law again! The Lord directed me that sowing yesterday wasn't enough; I had to keep looking for places to sow every day of my life.

When you see a brother in need, you're not supposed to say, "God bless you," and then turn and run the other way!

No, you're supposed to *do* something. Go help him. Sow a seed to meet his need.

With the Measure You Give

Our text goes on to say, "...**with the measure you deal out [with the measure you use when you confer benefits on others], it will be measured back to you**" (Luke 6:38).

What does that mean? Well, I describe it this way: If you sow in teaspoonfuls, you'll reap back a harvest measured in teaspoons. If you sow in cupfuls, you will receive multiplied cupfuls of blessings. But if you sow in barrels, then you will reap a multiplied harvest of barrel-sized blessings!

The Lord once used the following hypothetical situation to teach me this principle: An offering is about to be taken up in a church service. A man sits on the pew, wondering how much he should put in the offering. Meanwhile, the Lord sits on His throne, looking over the balcony of heaven at His child, waiting to see what he will do.

The man pulls out his checkbook, and the Lord speaks to his heart, giving him a figure to write out the check for. Then God tells His angels, "That's My boy! Angels, bring that barrel filled with blessings over to the open window." (Remember, in Malachi 3:10 God promised to pour you out blessings from the windows of heaven!)

Two huge angels lift a big, heavy barrel and carry it over to the open window of heaven. "All right, hold it right there," God says, and He looks down to see what His child is going to do.

In the meantime, this man thinks, *Man, I wonder if that figure is from the Lord. That's so much money; I don't know if I'll have enough left for my needs!*

183

Then the enemy comes along and gives him another, much smaller figure. The man can't decide which amount to write on the check—the larger amount or the smaller one. Then at the last minute, just as the offering plate passes by, he writes in the smaller amount.

The Father sadly says, "Take back the barrel and bring Me the teacup." God intended to give that man an outpouring of barrel-sized blessings, but the man's teacup-sized seed only produced a "teacup" harvest.

Let me explain the way this principle has worked in my life. When I began this lifestyle, I was only sowing one-dollar bills, so my harvest would come back to me in multiples of one dollar. When I started to give five-dollar bills, my harvest came back in multiples of five.

Finally I realized, *I seem to have tapped into something! I'm going to start giving ten-dollar bills every time there's an offering so I can increase my harvest.* Well, guess what? I began to reap in multiples of ten!

Little by little, I increased the measure of my seed from ten dollars, to twenty dollars, fifty dollars, and then one hundred dollars. Each time the measure increased, so did my harvest.

Then came the day when the Spirit of God said, "I want you to plant the biggest seed you've ever planted."

"How big, Lord? Two hundred dollars?"

"No, plant one thousand dollars."

I said, "Lord, I can't do that! This is the wrong time. I'm still in Bible school and I have a wife and three kids. We need that money and more besides!"

"That's the whole point," the Lord said. "What you have in your hand isn't enough for you anyway. In *your* hand, that thousand dollars won't go very far, but in My hand, it will!

Besides, in what measure do you want your harvest to return to you?"

"Big, Lord, I want my harvest to be *big*!"

"Well, then, you'll need to sow big."

So I obeyed. And ninety-seven days later, I received a check for $16,500 from a source I wouldn't have expected, dreamed of, or imagined in a million years!

Could God have given me the harvest of that check had I only planted five dollars in the offering? I doubt it, because I would have disobeyed the Lord's leading. You see, I was sowing big to my harvest in order for it to come back to me as it did—pressed down, shaken together, and running over!

Too many Christians sow *from* their harvest. "I wish I had a lot more money coming in," they say, "then I'd give more."

If that's the case, then decide how much money you want coming in; determine the amount of seed it will take to bring that size of harvest in, and then plant that seed accordingly.

"Oh, that can't be scriptural," some people think. Sure, it is! Remember, every farmer determines the size of his harvest at seedtime.

Let me give you an example. I have a friend named Roger who attends our Wisdom classes. Roger owns an accounting business. Now most business people focus their prayers on believing for more customers, more sales, more commissions, and higher salaries.

But after months of listening to the same principles of financial increase I'm teaching in this book, Roger prayed, "Lord, I see it now. You're in the seed-giving business! So I'm asking You for something different than I ever have before.

"Right now I'm giving $25 a month to three ministries each that teach the uncompromised Word and get people saved, delivered, and set free. Lord, I'm not going to ask You for more sales or greater profits; I want to ask You for more seed. My heart's desire is to give $100 a month to ten good ministries."

Seven months went by, and one night Roger came to the Wisdom class and gave his testimony. He said, "When I got my heart lined up with God's heart and became more interested in sowing than I was in building my business, my company exploded. Last month we were able to give $235 to seven different ministries!"

That's almost $2,000 in seed every month, when just seven months before Roger was only able to give $75!

You may ask, "How was that man able to do that?" God supernaturally increased Roger's business because he was more interested in multiplying his sowing than he was in multiplying his bank account.

So start changing your profit goals to sowing goals. If you're giving ten-dollar bills in the offerings, believe God for the ability to give twenty-dollar bills—then plant toward your harvest! If you want multiples of fifty dollars, then start sowing fifty-dollar offerings.

Friend, these principles of increase work. Anita and I are living testimonies to that fact. Every area of our lives—where we live, what we drive, what we eat, what we wear—has been transformed by the mystery of the kingdom that says *learn to sow*. Sowing has become a lifestyle for us, and we know that we always reap more than we sow.

When you come across someone with a need, you ought to be excited. You should say, "I know what's coming! My harvest is just around the corner, because I'm going to sow!"

When is that harvest coming? That's not your business. Your only job is to give, it's God's job to get the harvest to you in multiplied form!

Principle Number 3: You Always Reap In a Different Season

We know that reaping comes after sowing, but *when* does it come? The Bible answers that question and gives us the third principle of the law of seedtime and harvest: *You always reap in a different season than the one in which you sow.*

And let us not lose heart and grow weary and faint in acting nobly and doing right, for in due time and AT THE APPOINTED SEASON WE SHALL REAP, if we do not loosen and relax our courage and faint.

—Galatians 6:9

God says we reap *"in due time and at the appointed season."* That means the harvest doesn't always come when we want it. "But Lord," we cry, "I need my harvest *now*! Yes, Lord, now would be just about right." No, it comes *in due season.*

My own definition of *due season* is "never when the flesh wants it." Why? I say that because the flesh always wants everything *now.*

But God knows you planted seed, and He knows you have a harvest coming. He's faithful, so refuse to grow weary while waiting. Keep on sowing without "loosening or relaxing your courage"—even when you don't see any harvest on the horizon. As you're faithful to sow and "faint not," in due season you *will* see a harvest. You *must* because it's God's law.

So what does God mean when He says, "Don't grow weary in doing right"? When you grow weary, you get impatient. The harvest doesn't come as fast as you want it to, so you begin to doubt and say, "Nothing good ever happens to me. I never reap." But the very fact that God exhorts you not to grow weary lets you know the harvest won't necessarily come on your schedule.

We see the same message elsewhere in Scripture: **"Cast [or sow] your bread upon the waters, for you will find it AFTER MANY DAYS"** (Ecclesiastes 11:1).

In other words, get in on every opportunity you can find to give. As you sow, you *shall* reap even though it may be after "many days," or at the appointed season. (And notice that *you* must do the casting of your bread!)

Meanwhile, maintain your confession of faith. Say, "Blessings overtake me daily. I experience God's benefits every day of my life!"

You know, a farmer doesn't plant seed, for example, and then come back two days later and say, "Well, I tried planting, but it doesn't work. I went back and checked the seed, and there isn't anything coming up out of the ground." Farmers know better than to say that—but a lot of Christians don't!

Some Christians say, "I gave in the offering and then waited a whole week, but nothing happened!"

But just because you can't see any sprouts growing out of the ground right away doesn't nullify all the activity going on underneath the soil. Out of that seed a little root is fighting its way downward, and simultaneously, a tiny stalk is pushing its way upward out of the seed. The harvest is in the making; you just can't see it.

Sowing for Future Harvests

Another good definition of the phrase *due season* is "right when you need it." In other words, don't get frustrated because the reaping doesn't come as fast as you expected. God is never late, but He's also very rarely early! He gets your harvest to you right on time.

You see, the Bible says that a righteous man's steps are ordered of the Lord (Psalm 37:23). So if God has ordered your steps, it stands to reason that He knows what lies ahead in your future.

God knows more than you do about the future attacks of the enemy and also about what you will need in the future. Therefore, He may be trying to get across to you *where, when,* and *how much* to plant so your harvest comes at the appointed time—right when you need it in those future situations!

For instance, He may look into your future and say, "Okay, six months from now, I see that the enemy will attack My child's car. The engine is going to give out, and he'll need money to replace it or buy a new car. He doesn't know all this yet, but I see it coming.

"I don't want My child to suffer financially because of that future attack, so I'll prompt him to plant more seed right now. When that season comes, his harvest will be ready."

So the next time an offering plate comes around and the Lord speaks up in your spirit, "Forget that five-dollar bill. Plant more seed," don't answer, "Why, Lord? I don't need a big harvest. Everything is going great!"

Yes, but you don't know what the future holds. God's not telling you to plant more seed because He wants to get something *from* you. He's trying to tell you to sow more today, so a harvest will come *to* you to take care of these future needs!

We don't always know to prepare for the future, but God tells us to prepare by sowing: **"Give a portion to seven, yes, even [divide it] to eight, for you know not what evil may come upon the earth"** (Ecclesiastes 11:2).

You see, you don't know what evil may try to come into your life in the future, but God does. And despite every obstacle the enemy wants to place across your path in the days ahead, God always plans your future harvests!

So when you're in doubt about how much seed to sow, give the larger of the two figures you're juggling in your mind. As it says in this verse, if the figure is seven or eight, choose eight. The Lord may be telling you, "Sow more into your heavenly account now so the provision will be there when you need it in the future!"

God Reserves a Harvest Just for You

God actually appoints our harvesttime, according to Jeremiah 5:24: **"Let us now reverently fear and worship the Lord our God, Who gives rain, both the autumn and the spring rain in its season, WHO RESERVES AND KEEPS FOR US THE APPOINTED WEEKS OF THE HARVEST."**

God keeps track of the appointed weeks of your harvest. He reserves that harvest specifically for you, but you'll never see it if you grow weary in sowing before that harvest comes.

What if you never live a lifestyle of sowing? Well, someday you will stand before Jesus, and Jesus will say, "Child, do you see that big barn over there with your name on it? In that barn sit all the harvests I reserved for you in life. Unfortunately, the barn remains full. I kept trying to get your harvest to you throughout your life, but you were never faithful to plant your seed."

The Prayer of a Sower

Friend, you never have to hear Jesus say those sad words to you. Just make a commitment now to live by the law of seedtime and harvest. Then the many harvests God reserves for you in this life can arrive at the appointed times—*in due season!*

Let this prayer express your commitment to the Lord:

"Lord, I believe Your Word. I believe Your principles of increase. I believe that prosperity is in my hands, and this day I choose to obey Your Word.

"I thank You, Lord, that I now know the same mystery of the kingdom that You shared with the disciples. I'm going to do something with that mystery; I'm going to be a sower!

"I know that You are a God of multiplication. As I plant seed, I believe you will multiply it into a harvest of blessing in my life.

"Direct me this day and every day, Lord, how to sow. Speak to my heart and tell me where, when, and how much I should plant for the harvest You have prepared for me. In Jesus' Name, amen."

I believe now that you've prayed the prayer of a sower, your sowing will produce the reaping of harvests God has reserved for you—according to the three principles of seedtime and harvest!

Chapter 11
Watering the Seed
With the Tithe

"Bring all the tithes—the whole tenth of your income—into the storehouse, that there may be food in My house, and prove Me now by it, says the Lord of hosts, if I will not open the windows of heaven for you and pour you out a blessing, that there shall not be room enough to receive it."

—Malachi 3:10

Every seed you plant needs water to grow. We have talked about planting seed to expect a harvest, but if you never water the seed, your expected harvest will never come. So let's look at what causes those windows of heaven to open and its rains to water your seed.

My Personal Journey
In Learning To Tithe

I grew up Muslim, and somewhere in my upbringing I developed the idea that all Christian preachers were after people's money. So even after I got saved, I'd hang on to my wallet when I walked into church and wouldn't let go until I left!

When the offering bucket passed by, I'd pull out some bills and discreetly look for the smallest one I could find to put in.

It wasn't that I didn't have much money—I was a very successful businessman at the time—I just didn't think money had anything to do with God. In fact, the only reason I gave at all was that I didn't want to be noticed as the only one in church *not* putting something in the offering!

Despite my ignorance in the area of giving, I was hungry for God. One day as I prayed at home, I said, "Lord, I want more of You in my life!"

The Lord suddenly spoke to my spirit, saying, "Well, what are you doing with your money?"

"What does money have to do with anything, Lord?" I asked.

"Nasir, you've been robbing Me for years," the Lord replied. "When you put a few dollars in the offering, you're just 'tipping' Me. I don't want your tip."

"But, Lord, the pastor talks about paying tithes, or 10 percent of my income—and I made $112,000 last month! Ten percent of that is a lot of change! I mean, I think I've been doing good just to put five or ten dollars in the offering!

"Lord," I continued, "I really do love You. But unless You can prove to me from the Word that tithing is something I'm commanded to do, I'm just not going to write out that kind of check! However, if You can show me in Your Word that tithing is of You, I promise that for the rest of my life I will never rob You again."

So the Lord took me on a journey into His Word, searching for His kingdom principles tithing. What I found out in the Word that day radically changed my life. These principles, which I'm about to share with you, are the foundation upon which all other kingdom principles for financial increase are built.

Stop Robbing God

First, the Lord took me to Malachi 3, where He explains how to get closer to Him:

For I am the Lord, I do not change; that is why you, O sons of Jacob, are not consumed.

Even from the days of your fathers you have turned aside from My ordinances and have not kept them. Return to me, and I will return to you, says the Lord of hosts. But you say, How shall we return?

Will a man rob or defraud God? Yet you rob or defraud Me. But you say, In what way do we rob or defraud You? [You have withheld your] tithes and offerings.

You are cursed with the curse, for you are robbing Me, even this whole nation.

—Malachi 3:6-9

Here God says something profound to His people. Here's the essence: "From the days of your fathers, I gave you My Word. But instead of obeying My commandments, you turned aside from them. You stopped being doers of My Word. *Return to Me, and I will return to you.*"

God's command to "return" indicates that the nation of Israel needed to change directions. God wanted them to stop doing what they were doing, turn back toward God's Word and His ways, and do something different. And notice, the *people* had to do the turning before God returned to them.

So the Israelites asked, "But *how* do we return to You, Lord?"

That's a good question and one we need to ask. The Lord asks the same thing of us. "Do you want to get closer to Me? Then take the first step and obey My Word. If you take the first step, I'll take the next and draw close to you."

"Okay, Lord, I'm ready," I can hear a Christian praying. "I'm hungry for more of You. So what's the first step? Should I read my Bible more? Should I pray more, worship more, attend church more? How can I get closer to You, Lord?"

"Get closer to Me through your wallet."

"Oh, no, Lord, not through my wallet! I'll get closer to you in any way but that one!"

But God answers, "That's exactly why your money is the first thing I'm dealing with. Don't tell Me you want to get closer to Me if you let your money stand between us."

Would God say something like that? He just did in this passage in Malachi! He told His people, "You've been robbing Me."

The first time I read that, it made no sense to me. I asked God, "Lord, how can a man rob You? What is he going to do —walk up to You and say, 'Uh, excuse me, God, but this is a stick-up'? A person would have to be crazy to think he could try to rob You. I certainly would never do it."

The Lord said, "Yet you *have* unwittingly robbed Me, Nasir, by withholding your tithes and offerings."

Once I understood this, I got on my knees and repented. I hadn't realized what I was doing to the Creator of heaven and earth—the One who saved, delivered, and healed me. At that moment I determined I would never rob God again.

If we don't change in the area of giving, we may as well forget about trying to get closer to God in other ways because our wallets will stop us! God doesn't want a part of us; He wants *all* of us.

Getting Out From Under The Curse of Poverty

Let's look again at Malachi 3:9. It says, **"Ye are cursed with a curse; for ye have robbed Me...."** *(KJV)*. The nation of Israel brought upon themselves the curse of poverty by not being faithful with their tithes and offerings. That's also the case with the body of Christ today.

Many are broke and crying out for money, but in a sense, God can't do anything. He says, "I want to bless you, but you're living under a curse. Get out from under that curse, or My blessings can never overtake you."

You see, God doesn't put curses on anyone, people reap the harvest of their own actions—whether curses or blessings.

Even in the natural realm, stealing from someone brings consequences. Suppose a man robs a bank and then gets caught. When he stands before the judge, the judge decrees, "Your sentence is five years in jail."

What if the thief said, "Judge, I'm a nice guy. You're a nice guy. I never did anything to you, so why are you sending me to jail?"

The judge would reply, "I don't have anything against you personally. For all I know, you may be a nice guy. But I'm sending you to jail to reap the consequences of your actions." You see, the law, "Whatever you sow you will reap," governs the earth.

Likewise, Israel brought itself under the curse of poverty because that is the consequences people reap when they rob God. Spiritually, it's like going to "jail." But God didn't put Israel under that curse; their own disobedience did.

The situation isn't much better among God's people today. Somewhere between 6 and 15 percent of believers in America tithe. Even if we assume that the larger figure is correct, that still means 85 percent of the Christians in this country place themselves under the curse of poverty by neglecting to tithe.

Those Christians may think, *God wants me poor.* But in actuality, God loves them and wants them to prosper. The truth is, they are simply experiencing the consequences of a law that governs the universe—they curse themselves by robbing God.

But God in His mercy provides our way out from under the curse of poverty!

Bring the Tithe Into the Storehouse

Verse 10 holds the key to releasing us from the curse of poverty: **"Bring all the tithes (the whole tenth of your income) into the storehouse, that there may be food in My house, and prove Me now by it, says the Lord of hosts, if I will not open the windows of heaven for you and pour you out a blessing, that there shall not be room enough to receive it."**

This is the only time in the entire Bible that God says, "Go ahead—check Me out. Prove Me." It's interesting that the one time He tells us to prove Him, it is in connection with paying tithes and offerings.

I did some intensive research on what the tithe is. (I had to for my own sake. I wasn't going to write an $11,200 tithe check unless I knew it was God telling me to do it!) A tithe means one-tenth of all your income—not one-twentieth, not the smallest or the largest bill in your pocket, but one-tenth.

And it isn't just *any* tenth of your income either. It's the *first* tenth. In other words, you set aside a tenth to God before you partake of your income. The Bible says, **"Honor the Lord with your possessions, and WITH THE FIRSTFRUITS OF ALL YOUR INCREASE"** (Proverbs 3:9 NKJV).

People ask me, "Well, does that mean the first tenth of my net income or my gross income?"

I tell them, "Well, what kind of blessing do you want—a net or a gross blessing? I can tell you how I feel about it. If there were any question in my mind about the matter, I'd rather be *over* the amount I'm supposed to tithe than *under*. Removing the curse is too important to me."

Suppose when you stand before Jesus, you ask, "Should I have tithed on the net or the gross?" Even if He replies, "You need only tithe on the net," what's the big deal?

You might exclaim, "You mean, I gave 2 percent extra all of my life by tithing on my gross income, Lord!"

"Yes," Jesus would answer, "but I took that 2 percent as seed, multiplied it, and poured it back into your life as harvest."

So even if you pay too much in tithes, it will only mean a greater harvest for you if you do it in faith. You just can't lose by deciding to give more instead of less to God's kingdom!

God Will Open the Windows of Heaven

The Lord once said to me, "As long as My children continue to tip Me instead of pay their tithes, they'll never experience My windows of heaven opening over their finances."

Only one other time does the Bible talk about God's opening the windows of heaven. It says that in the days of Noah, God opened those windows and heaven's rains flooded the planet for forty days and nights (Genesis 7:11,12). That proves that heaven's windows are extremely large and *a lot* of water pours out of them! So if we want to open those windows for an outpouring of blessings in our lives, we must be faithful to tithe, not tip, God.

You see, the tithe belongs to the Lord. We're going to look at a Scripture later that proves that fact, but for right now, get ahold of this: When you pay your tithes, you simply return what already belongs to God. Therefore, your tithe can't be your seed. The tithe doesn't operate according to the seedtime and harvest law.

What is your seed? Your offering. However, you can't plant offerings and expect God to multiply them if you're not paying your tithes.

Your purpose in being faithful to tithe is to open the windows of heaven so God's spiritual rains can water your seed. On the other hand, if you're not faithful to tithe, the seed you sow will fall on dry, barren ground. Deprived of God's life-giving rains of blessing and power, that seed will die without ever producing a harvest.

Bring Your Tithes to God's Storehouse

Notice that God says to *bring* the tithes into His storehouse. That does *not* mean "Send your tithes in the mail as you stay home from church sleeping late."

God doesn't want you to forsake assembling together with other believers (Hebrews 10:25). He wants you up out of bed, at the local church where you are fed the Word, and paying your tithes! For you, your local church *is* God's storehouse!

"But I don't have time to go to church," you say. Then you need to make time. The truth is, time isn't the issue—your priorities are the issue. When church becomes important enough to you, you'll make the time for it.

God Will Rebuke the Devourer

Not only does God open windows of financial blessing to us, but we receive added benefits as we faithfully tithe:

"AND I WILL REBUKE THE DEVOURER for your sakes, so that he will not destroy the fruit of your ground, nor shall the vine fail to bear fruit for you in the field," says the Lord of hosts.
—Malachi 3:11 NKJV

Does money seem to flow out faster than it comes in because of unexpected expenses? For example, you think you're doing well financially, and then all of a sudden the car, the washing machine, and the dishwasher all break down the same week! What's happening? That's the devourer stealing the fruit of your labor.

How can you stop the devourer? Be faithful with your tithes and offerings! Your faithfulness allows God to move on your behalf and rebuke the devourer. Almighty God personally tells the devil to back off and leave you alone!

Don't Rob God of His Pleasure

I studied this passage of Scripture in Malachi 3, and one thing bothered me. I said, "Lord, there's something I don't understand. As I've been going through the Scriptures, I've found proof that the tithe belongs to You [see Leviticus 27:30].

"You stated in Malachi 3:8 that people rob You in both tithes *and* offerings, but I haven't found any Scripture that says offerings belong to You. As far as I can tell, offerings are our seed, planted by our own free will in any amount we choose by Your leading. So how do we rob You when we don't plant our seed?"

The Lord answered my question by showing me another principle in the Word: **"Let the Lord be magnified, Who takes pleasure in the prosperity of His servant"** (Psalm 35:27). Then He said, "When you don't give offerings, you rob Me of My pleasure and joy in seeing you blessed."

When I heard that, I determined then and there that I'd never rob God of His joy again by not giving offerings. I purposed to do everything in my power to make Him happy, planting plenty of seed so He could multiply it into a great harvest of blessings!

All We Are and Have Is the Lord's

Then God showed me an interesting Scripture: **"For the [whole] earth is the Lord's and everything that is in it"** (1 Corinthians 10:26).

"What?" I exclaimed. "Are You telling me, Lord, that everything in this earth is already Yours, including me and everything I own—even my entire bank account?"

"That's right." He answered. "I give you food on your table, the car you drive, money in the bank, and job promotions. I give you the very air you breathe. *Everything* you are and everything you have, I give to you. But I'll allow you to keep 90 percent if you'll stop robbing Me."

"Lord, I'm so sorry I tipped You. I won't ever rob You again! In fact, paying You 10 percent of my income is starting to look pretty good!"

I guarantee you, once you understand that God gives you everything you own, you won't be so stingy with the 10 percent that belongs to Him!

Next, the Lord took me to the Scripture that showed that the tithe belongs to the Lord:

And ALL OF THE TITHE of the land, whether of the seed of the land or of the fruit of the tree, IS THE LORD'S; it is holy to the Lord.
—Leviticus 27:30

Did you notice that Israel had no option here? It says that "*all* of the tithe of the land" belongs to the Lord. That's why God said His people robbed Him; they hadn't returned to Him what was already His!

You see, we can't *give* God the tithe, because that would imply that we once owned that 10 percent. We're not doing

203

God any favors when we pay our tithe; we are simply returning to God what always belonged to Him—not us—in the
first place.

The tithe never belonged to us and never will. God does-
n't change (Malachi 3:6). Therefore, returning the tithe to
God brings us out from under the curse of poverty and places
us under the open windows of heaven.

If we decide to keep the tithe, we put ourselves in serious
trouble. Number one, we rob Almighty God Himself. Number
two, we put ourselves under the curse of poverty. And number three, we pay God 20 percent interest on His money!

"Pay God interest on the tithe?" You say, "That sounds a
little farfetched!" But I'm not the one who said it; *God* said it!
The Bible says, **"And if a man wants to redeem [or keep]
any of his tithe, he shall add a fifth [or 20 percent] to
it"** (Leviticus 27:31).

"But why do I have to pay interest to God?" you ask. You
do for the same reason you pay interest on money borrowed
from the bank—the money isn't yours. But in the case of the
tithe, you are borrowing *God's* money.

Actually, the real issue is not that God charges you interest, but when you don't tithe you open the door for the devil
to steal your finances!

A woman once said to me, "This month I'm having some
financial difficulties, and I can't tithe because I have to pay
my credit card bill. If I don't pay that bill, I'm going to be in
big trouble."

Isn't it interesting! That woman feared the credit card
company more than she feared God! But the truth is not "I
can't afford to tithe"—it's "I can't afford *not* to tithe"! The
money simply isn't ours to keep.

The Tithe Is Holy

Notice that Leviticus 27:30 also says that the tithe is holy to the Lord. God so highly esteems the tithe that He calls it holy! How can we therefore possibly look on the tithe with any less esteem?

If God considers the tithe holy, we should consider it holy as well. Only holy hands should touch it—the hands of those obedient to God's Word.

In the Old Testament, when the wrong people touched the holy things consecrated unto the Lord, they died (1 Chronicles 13:9,10). Obviously, we need to take it seriously when God declares something holy.

Incidentally, this is also an important consideration for those who serve as ushers in their church, because if an usher puts himself under the curse of poverty by robbing God, he shouldn't handle the church's holy tithe. He needs to repent before God and commit to bring his tithes into God's storehouse!

The tithe is serious. Dr. Yongghi Cho, the South Korean pastor of the largest church in the world, takes the tithe very seriously—and he has more than 750,000 members, so he's doing something right! Dr. Cho's church members have access to lists of those who tithe. That way they can ensure doing business with tithers.

For instance, one of Dr. Cho's church members may decide, "I want to ask a certain brother to work with me in my business, but first I'm going to check his tithing records. If he's not a tither, I don't want to do business with someone who lives under a curse!"

So the next time you put your tithe in the offering plate, don't just casually drop it in. Your tithe is holy unto the Lord, and it belongs to Him. Treat it with reverence.

Tithing Is a Commandment

God wants to promote His people, but believers can't receive God's promotion until they fulfill God's commandment and tithe:

> **Then you shall say before the Lord your God, I HAVE BROUGHT THE HALLOWED THINGS (THE TITHE) out of my house and moreover have given them to the Levite, to the stranger and the sojourner, to the fatherless, and to the widow, ACCORDING TO ALL YOUR COMMANDMENTS WHICH YOU HAVE COMMANDED ME; I have not transgressed any of Your commandments, neither have I forgotten them.**
> **...And He will make you high above all nations which He has made, in praise and in fame and in honor, and that you shall be a holy people to the Lord your God, as He has spoken.**
> —Deuteronomy 26:13,19

Under the New Covenant, the local church uses the tithe to pay for furthering the Gospel. This includes building expenses, pastoral salaries, benevolent expenses, evangelistic outreaches, and so forth.

Under the Old Covenant, the use of the tithe was also for the furtherance of God's kingdom. For example, the tithe met the material needs of the Levites (who were equivalent to ministers today) and others in need, such as widows, orphans, and poor strangers in the land (v. 13).

Again, this verse tells us that the tithe is hallowed, or holy. It also says that tithing isn't optional; it's a *divine commandment*. We don't tithe according to the Lord's *suggestions*, but according to His *commandments*.

A believer might say, "I just got my paycheck, but I'm not sure I'm going to write my tithe check this week." No, don't even think like that! Tithing is not an option. Although you might argue with a pastor who says you're supposed to tithe, you can't argue with God's Word!

"But I just can't afford to tithe!" another person might protest. That is a lie from the pit of hell. God is just and doesn't give you commandments you can't fulfill. Fulfilling His commandments is important. In fact, Jesus compares our love for Him with keeping His commandments: **"If you [really] love Me, you will keep (obey) My commands"** (John 14:15).

You see, the verb *love* is active, not passive. In other words, when you love someone, you show it. The way you show your love for God is by doing His commandments, and that includes tithing.

Yet some people maintain the attitude, "Lord, I love You with every part of me except my money." No, God can't be the God of your life but not your money. Make up your mind—if you make Him God of your life, make Him Lord of *every* part of it.

"But it's so tough to tithe!" others say. According to the Bible, that excuse doesn't work:

For the [true] love of God is this: that we do His commands [keep His ordinances and are mindful of His precepts and teaching]. And these orders of His are not irksome (burdensome, oppressive, or grievous).

—1 John 5:3

Do you want to show God you love Him? Then do His Word. His commandments are never too hard, and He will never ask you to do something you don't have the ability to do. His commandments are not hard, oppressive, or burdensome.

And God is faithful to bless your obedience! I can't begin to tell you the testimonies we receive from people who take God at His Word and as a result experience financial miracles. They've committed themselves to tithe no matter what, and God honors their obedience to His Word.

For instance, one woman heard this teaching and decided from that day forward she would be a tither. She prayed, "Lord, I don't know how I'm going to do it. Every penny of my paycheck is already accounted for. But You said to prove You on the tithe, so that's what I'm going to do!"

So she started tithing. One, two, and then three weeks went by. Standing in faith, the woman refused to look at her bank account balance, because she knew she would need rent at the end of the month and didn't want a dwindling balance to tempt her not to tithe. Regardless of how impossible her financial situation looked, she faithfully continued to tithe every week.

Three days before the end of the month—right as her rent was due—the windows of heaven opened for this woman. Her boss called her into his office and gave her a $10,000 salary increase! This woman's obedience to tithe, even when it seemed hard to do, turned out to be her key to financial breakthrough!

Tithe Comes First, Reward Second

That woman's testimony manifests God's promise in His Word:

And the Levite [because he has no part or inheritance with you] and the stranger or temporary resident, and the fatherless and the widow who are in your towns shall come and eat and be satisfied, so that THE LORD YOUR GOD MAY BLESS YOU IN ALL THE WORK OF YOUR HANDS THAT YOU DO.

—Deuteronomy 14:29

Everyone loves the promise in that verse. "Hallelujah!" they say, "God's going to bless me in all the work of my hands!" But that promise doesn't apply to you unless you've fulfilled verse 22: **"You shall SURELY tithe all the yield of your seed [or grain] produced by your field each year."**

The woman whose testimony I've shared determined that she would *surely* tithe, no matter what—and God was faithful to do His part by blessing her in all the work of her hands! But notice that obedience came before the reward.

Another Scripture shows us the great increase we can expect from the tithe:

Honor the Lord with your capital and sufficiency [from righteous labors] and with the firstfruits of all your income; so shall your storage places be filled with plenty....

—Proverbs 3:9,10

Today the phrase *storage places* usually refers to our bank accounts.

So how would you like to see your bank account filled with plenty? Once again, in order to receive the promise in verse 10, you must obey the condition in verse 9: Honor the Lord by giving Him the firstfruits of all your increase.

Tithing in the New Testament

You may say, "That's all fine, Nasir, but we live under the New Covenant. What does the New Testament say about tithing?" Let's take a look: **"Here** [on earth] **mortal men receive tithes, but there** [in heaven] **he receives them, of whom it is witnessed that he lives"** (Hebrews 7:8 NKJV).

The writer of Hebrews spoke of Jesus, the One **"of whom it is witnessed that he lives."** Jesus is the High Priest of our profession (Hebrews 3:1). Another verse also refers to Jesus as our High Priest: **"...We have such a High Priest, One Who is seated at the right hand of the majestic [God] in heaven"** (Hebrews 8:1).

Verse 3 goes on to say, **"For every high priest is appointed to offer up gifts and sacrifices; so it is essential for this [High Priest] to have some offering to make also."** You see, Jesus as our High Priest receives our tithes and offerings and presents them to the Father. Unfortunately, too often He goes into the throne room empty-handed!

Tithing as a Form of Worship

We've discovered that the Lord considers tithing holy. Scripture tells us He also considers it a form of worship:

> **And now, behold, I bring the firstfruits of the ground which You, O Lord, have given me. And you shall set it down before the Lord your God and worship before the Lord your God.**
> —Deuteronomy 26:10

That's why you just can't play around with the tithe. In your obedience to bring Him your firstfruits, you acknowledge that God is your Source, the One who gave you every-thing you have. Therefore, when you bring your tithe to church and set it down before the Lord, you do it as worship to Him.

After listening to me teach on tithing, the pastor of a church realized its importance as part of worship. He was so impressed with this truth that one night he walked up to the pulpit and told his congregation, "I want to ask you to forgive me.

"Many of you have come to me in the past and said you were going through a hard time financially. You told me that you couldn't afford to tithe, and I told you it was all right. Or you said you could only give 5 percent instead of 10, and I said that was all right.

"I repent of every time I ever said that, because I allowed you to stay under a curse all these years.

"Please forgive me," the pastor continued. "I was wrong. I hadn't realized that the tithe was not yours to begin with and that you were actually withholding something that belongs to God. I will never compromise the Word again.

"So if you ever come to me and say you can't afford to tithe, I'm going to tell you to sell your car and walk before you rob God. God will provide you with the transportation you need, but you can't afford *not* to tithe."

My respect for that pastor increased tremendously as I listened to him. Here was a man humble enough to admit he had been wrong. He humbled himself so his sheep wouldn't have to stay in poverty any longer. And he emphasized by his public repentance the importance of the tithe to worship.

Choose Life

You and I have a choice. We can live under the enemy's curses or in God's blessings.

I call heaven and earth to witness this day against you that I have set before you life and death, THE BLESSINGS and THE CURSES; therefore CHOOSE LIFE that you and your descendants may live.
—Deuteronomy 30:19

God won't force us to do anything, including rendering to Him the tithe—even though it belongs to Him! If we don't want to tithe, we don't have to.

But making wrong choices in life—choosing not to tithe, for example—causes us to live under the curse of the law from which we've already been redeemed. It's never God's choice that we suffer lack; He doesn't bless some and leave others broke. In a sense, *we* choose to suffer lack.

Poverty comes upon us as a curse when we don't obey the Word with our finances, because we reap what we sow (Galatians 6:7). Another way to say it is that **"your dealings will return upon your own head"** (Obadiah 1:15).

Therefore, in tithing, God always leaves the choice up to you. Will you rob God, or will you return the tithe that rightly belongs to Him? Will you live under the curse of poverty or walk in God's blessings? Will you choose life or embrace death?

If you choose cursings and disobedience—death—His hands are tied; He can't help you. As the Word says, your dealings will return upon your own head!

God sets before you the choice and tells you, "You choose: life or death, blessings or cursings." And He's such a loving

God that He then gives us the right answer: "Choose the way of My blessings—choose life!"

The Tither's Prayer

Don't let the enemy steal your harvest any longer. If you've been unfaithful in tithing in the past, God provides for your forgiveness through the blood of His Son Jesus: "**If we confess our sins, he is faithful and just to forgive us our sins, and to cleanse us from all unrighteousness**" (1 John 1:9 KJV).

God is so good that if you repent, He will completely erase all the times you robbed Him of the tithe so you can begin with a clean slate. In fact, He's such a good God that when you make a decision to give Him what is rightfully His, He will also bless you on credit!

God will take you at your word. Commit to start tithing to open those windows of heaven before your first tithe check ever hits the offering plate!

If you're sick and tired of living under the curse of poverty, this is your moment to take off those chains of financial bondage once and for all. Pray this prayer from your heart, and get ready for a financial breakthrough!

"Father God, I have learned from Your Word the importance of the tithe, and I believe it. I choose this day to believe Your kingdom principles, not the lies of the enemy.

"I know my tithe is holy to You. So I proclaim that from this day forward, I will always worship You with my tithe, the firstfruits of my income. As I am faithful to return to You the tithe which already belongs to You, I know You'll be faithful to open the windows of heaven for me.

"I know I don't have to live under the curse of poverty anymore, but according to Your Word, You will pour out Your rain on my seed and multiply a harvest of blessings so great that I won't have room enough to receive it!

"Thank You, Father, for that harvest. I receive it now by faith! In the Name of Jesus I pray, amen."

Friend, I rejoice with you that through your obedience to tithe, you've now opened the windows of heaven over your financial life!

Chapter 12
How To Reap Your Harvest

"But when the grain is ripe and permits, immediately he sends forth [the reapers] and puts in the sickle, because the harvest stands ready."

—Mark 4:29

Cultivating the growth of a seed involves more than just planting and watering. The farmer sows the seed, and takes his sickle out to the field to reap the harvest. But if he neglects to reap his harvest, the fruit of it will be lost, left dying on the vine.

Let's look at some scriptural guidelines on how to reap the harvest from all the seed you've planted over the years. No one knows better than the Chief Husbandman Himself how to bring in your full harvest in due time and at the appointed season.

The Harvest Comes
To Those Who Believe

The first thing to understand is that the harvest doesn't come to everyone who sows seed into the kingdom of God; it only comes to those who *believe:* "**The word which they**

[the Israelites] heard did not profit them, NOT BEING MIXED WITH FAITH in those who heard it" (Hebrews 4:2 NKJV).

The Israelites heard the good news that God wanted to deliver them from bondage and give them the Promised Land, but the message they heard didn't benefit them because it was not mixed with faith.

Now apply that same example to the law of sowing and reaping. Here's what I mean. I know people who just toss money in an offering plate as it goes by them with no clue of the significance of what they're doing. Those people cannot reap a harvest from their seed because they do not mix their sowing with faith.

Plant your seed into the kingdom of God with *full expectancy* of the harvest the Word promises! As you place that envelope containing your seed into the offering plate, release your faith as well.

Tell the Lord specifically what you're believing Him to provide so that you will know when your harvest has come. For instance, you might say, "Lord, according to Your Word, I'm planting this seed towards my rent being paid. Thank You, Lord, for the harvest!"

Bring in Your Harvest by Faith

The truth is, you reap finances the same way you reap any other promise of God. First, you *believe* God's promise in your heart, and second, you release your faith by *speaking* what you believe (Romans 10:8,9). That's how you were first saved, and that's how you receive every promise in God's Word.

God is the One who multiplies your sowing, but *you* must exercise your faith to reap your financial harvest. *You* cause increase to manifest in your life.

How do you do that? First, meditate on kingdom principles regarding financial increase. Focus your thoughts and attention on these truths until they become more real on the inside of you than the circumstances you face on the outside.

Once you believe in your heart that it is God's will to prosper you and that His laws of sowing and reaping work, then apply His principles of increase to your life: live a lifestyle of sowing and tithing. As you do, you obtain the legal right to a financial harvest.

Now walk in that legal right. Release your faith by calling in your harvest with the words of your mouth: "Lord, I'm a tither, and I've planted seed into Your kingdom. I believe Your Word, so right now I claim the harvest that is rightfully mine!

"Angels, go forth and bring in my harvest! The Word says men shall give back into my bosom, so angels, I commission you to go forth and influence men to give to me. Thank You, Lord, for my harvest!"

You may say, "Wait a minute! Where did you get this idea of angels' influencing men?" Well, have you ever observed the influence of demons on a person? If demons can influence people for evil, certainly, angels can likewise influence people for good.

You see, ministering angels surround you, waiting to hearken to the voice of the Word (Psalm 103:20). Hebrews 1:14 says that they are **"ministering spirits sent forth to minister for those who will inherit salvation"** (NKJV).

When you release your faith and pray the Word, your angels say, "Oh, he just spoke the Word! I have to go—I've got a harvest to bring in!"

What if you start speaking words of doubt, saying things like, "This seedtime and harvest business doesn't work"? Your angels would say, "He just canceled his order, so now we can't do anything about his harvest."

You see, angels only speak one language—the language of the Word. They do not respond to crying, screaming, whining, or complaining, but only to the Word spoken forth in faith.

Between 'Amen' And 'There It Is!'

How often do you release your faith and send forth the angels to bring in the harvest you've believed for? If you pray the prayer of faith twice for the same need, then you obviously didn't believe what you prayed the first time.

You may wonder what to do between the "amen" and the "there it is!" The time between when you call in the harvest and when you actually see it manifested in your life. Simply this: you stir up your faith.

The Bible says to "stir up the gift of God which is in you" (2 Timothy 1:6). *In other words, the supernatural force of faith exists inside you and you must stir it up.* Therefore, if you believe you received your harvest when you prayed, stir up your faith and *keep* it stirred up! You do that by *thinking* faith, *talking* faith, and *thanking* God in faith for the answer!

When negative thoughts come to mind, replace them with thoughts that line up with the Word. Instead of thinking, *It's been a long time, and I don't see the harvest,* start dwelling on faith Scriptures. Think to yourself, *I'm a covenant child of*

God. My God shall supply all my needs according to His riches in glory because I'm a giver!

Every time you open your mouth to speak, talk about the harvest you believe is coming in. Don't talk about your lack, and *don't* say that sowing seed doesn't work. Just keep speaking God's Word over your finances, and soon you'll get your faith so stirred up about your incoming harvest that you won't be able to contain your excited expectation of it! Then every time you think of it, thank God that your harvest is already on the way. Thank Him for His faithfulness to always meet your needs.

The more you thank God, the more quickly your harvest manifests, because that's your faith speaking. God says that faith is the *substance* of what you're hoping for or looking forward to, and the *evidence* of what you do not yet see (Hebrews 11:1).

So start praising God! Don't wait until your harvest manifests to praise Him, but praise Him in faith for the financial breakthroughs already coming your way.

Keep Your Mouth Hooked Up to Your Harvest

Why is it so important to speak your faith? Jesus explained, our mouths are hooked up to our harvest:

Truly I tell you, whoever says to this mountain, Be lifted up and thrown into the sea and does not doubt at all in his heart but believes that what he says will take place, it will be done for him.
—Mark 11:23

Get ahold of this truth: *You sow with your giving, and you reap with your words.*

The moment you plant your seed and release your faith with the words of your mouth, the angels begin working to bring in the finances and your harvest is on its way!

You can either hinder or help your harvest manifest by what you allow your mouth to say. Words of doubt cancel the delivery of your harvest while words of faith bring your harvest into manifestation.

There is a powerful force behind saying and believing that brings every promise of God into your life. But to allow that force to work, *you cannot change what you believe, nor what you say* as you wait for your harvest to manifest.

As the Bible says, you hold the power of life and death in your tongue (Proverbs 18:21). Therefore, with your words you can kill your harvest or bring it to life.

The truth is, more harvests have been left on the heavenly shelf as a result of believers' negative confessions than any other reason.

Therefore, no matter what, maintain this confession of faith: "Thank You, Lord, the harvest is coming. My bills are already taken care of. I know it's done because I've planted the seed, and I have every right to expect the harvest. I thank You, Lord, that the angels are now bringing in the harvest. The harvest is coming! *It's coming!*"

Then you must believe you've received your answer from God. As the Bible says, **"Whatever you ask for in prayer, believe (trust and be confident) that it is granted to you, and you will [get it]"** (Mark 11:24).

In other words, believe you've already received your harvest and that it's on the way. When do you believe? When you don't yet see the harvest!

For instance, suppose you are believing God for a new van. After you've asked Him for it and planted seeds toward it, then any time you think of it, say to yourself, "My new van is coming in. It's gorgeous, loaded with all the extras I've asked God for. It's already mine; I can see it, and I know it because I planted the seed and did not doubt. I rest in faith now, and rejoice over my harvest!"

You see, if you really believe you received your harvest *when you prayed*, you will rejoice right now—*not* when you actually see the manifestation of your harvest.

You may say, "When I see my harvest, then I'll rejoice."

But if that's your attitude, you didn't believe you received your answer at the time you prayed. If you believed, then every word out of your mouth would speak of the harvest in the past tense, because it has already been released in the spirit realm.

You would say, "I sent forth my angels, and I believe they're bringing in my harvest right now. I know that van is coming in. Thank You, God, for my van!"

Many Christians plant seed without ever seeing their harvest. But here's the good news: Unlike natural seed, spiritual seed never dies, nor does it have a time limit in which to germinate, grow, and produce a harvest.

Every seed you ever planted represents a harvest just waiting in heaven for you to call into your life by faith. So if you canceled out your harvest in the past with words of doubt and unbelief, repent and ask God to forgive you. Then release your faith once again, and commission the angels to bring in your unclaimed harvests!

Receive the Harvest
Through Faith and Patience

When you plant seed, you must believe it will bear fruit in order for it to actually do so. But harvesting that fruit takes patience as well as faith. Jesus spoke of this process of believing for the harvest in His parable of a farmer:

> **The kingdom of God is like a man who scatters seed upon the ground, and then continues sleeping and rising night and day while the seed sprouts and grows and increases—he knows not how.**
> **The earth produces [acting] by itself—first the blade, then the ear, then the full grain in the ear.**
> —Mark 4:26-28

Notice the farmer in Jesus' parable plants seed but has no idea how the harvest actually comes. Nonetheless, he doesn't let that concern him; he is the "good ground" Jesus described in the parable of the sower:

> **But as for that [seed] in the good soil, these are [the people] who, hearing the Word, hold it fast in a just (noble, virtuous) and worthy heart, and steadily BRING FORTH FRUIT WITH PATIENCE.**
> —Luke 8:15

After you sow the seed into the ground, don't walk off and start worrying about it. Follow the farmer's example—he's so sure of God's law of sowing and reaping that he goes to bed and falls asleep! He knows the seed automatically increases according to God's law of seedtime and harvest, and that whether he is asleep or awake, the seed *will* grow.

Although the farmer doesn't see the results of his planting the first, second, or third week, he doesn't panic. In fact, he keeps on sleeping and rising, patiently going about his daily life. He doesn't know *how* his seed sprouts and grows; all he knows is that the law of seedtime and harvest works. He simply waits patiently and in faith.

So don't worry about your harvest. Just plant your seed and then enter into rest (Hebrews 4:3)! Through faith *and patience* you inherit God's promises (Hebrews 6:12).

In other words, don't try to decide when it's harvesttime; let *God* do that. Remember, when you plant seed, you reap your harvest in a different season.

If you say, "But I planted seed three days ago, and I haven't seen a harvest yet!" let me reassure you—that's all right. Just relax, and be patient without doubting.

And if you say, "Now it's been a whole year, and still no harvest," the message remains the same. Have patience without doubting. Let patience have her *perfect* work (James 1:4). Why? Because God promises you will reap in due season!

For example, my wife and I planted seeds to help others buy their homes ten years before we owned our own home outright. Now we *thought* we needed to own a home years before we actually did, but God knew we'd be moving to the United States (we had no idea at the time!). He knew that the appointed season for our "home harvest" was to be in the States.

During the long years between the sowing and the harvest, Anita and I exercised patience without doubting that our home was on the way. We had to practice what we preach!

I know it's tempting during that "in-between" time to say, "I sure wish God would hurry up." But God knows you need that harvest. He has your situation under control, and He'll get that harvest to you in time.

"Yes, but in four more days, I have to pay rent!" you complain. Don't you think God knows that? He'll get it to you if you refuse to get anxious and full of worry.

Do you really believe in the God of multiplication? Do you believe in His law of sowing and reaping? If you do, then you can rest, knowing God will multiply your seed back to you.

So sleep peacefully tonight and every other night. And remember, you bring forth your harvest by faith and patience.

Only God Knows How Your Harvest Will Come

Let's observe something else about the harvest from a verse we've already studied:

He who observes the wind [and waits for all conditions to be favorable] will not sow, and he who regards the clouds will not reap.

—Ecclesiastes 11:4

What does the last part of that verse mean, "*...he who regards the clouds will not reap*"? Literally, it means if you're a farmer watching the clouds, you may say, "Oh, it looks like a storm is coming, so I won't go out to the fields to reap the harvest today."

That may work in the natural realm, but in the spiritual realm, there is never a time to stop standing in faith for your harvest.

Therefore, don't be moved by the stormy circumstances of life as you wait for your harvest. Know that your seed has produced a harvest because you have sown and you have a covenant with God for blessing. And keep thanking Him for the harvest that is coming in by faith!

"Yes, but I planted last week, and no money has come in yet," someone says. "I didn't get a raise, and I found no check in the mailbox."

If you're looking for external circumstances to confirm what you believe, you'll never reap a harvest. Stop looking at the clouds, trying to decide when, how, and through whom God will bring in the harvest.

Just like the farmer in the parable of Mark 4, rest in faith that something's happening in your seed beneath the ground even though your natural eyes can't see a thing. Walking by faith means believing God for the harvest when you can't see how your answer can come to pass.

At one time or another we've all wondered, *How is my seed going to be multiplied? What avenue will God use to get it back to me? Will I get a raise at my job? Will that businessman at church give me the money I need?*

But instead, we need to stay in peace and not worry about the harvest, knowing God will take care of bringing it to us as we rest in faith.

Another problem about trying to figure out how your harvest will come in is that you can easily become a respecter of persons. *I think I'd better be really nice to that brother,* you may think. *He may be the one God is going to use to get my harvest to me.*

Don't limit God with your carnal speculations! There's a 99.99 percent chance that you're wrong, because you just don't know who God will use as a channel for your harvest.

It seems like God orchestrates a spiritual "chess game," moving people's seed and harvest around in a way that best benefits everyone concerned.

Although in the natural it may look as if your harvest should come from a particular person, God may use a totally unexpected source. For example, many times God has used an unsaved person—the *last* person Anita and I would ever expect to receive from—to give us needed finances or material goods.

Our harvest of $16,500 was one such time—the time I obeyed God's prompting and sowed in thousands, thereby reaping in thousands. We would never have imagined receiving money from the particular person who gave it to us—especially since we were in the ministry serving God and this person didn't even know Jesus!

So let me encourage you. Don't stay up all night biting your nails, worrying about where the harvest will come from. Let God figure it out. After all, He's a God of order. He's not confused, and He knows what He's doing!

On the other hand, if God tells *you* to give to someone, make sure you obey. God can't get your harvest to you until you sow, because remember, you're not just a receiver of harvest; you're a *giver* of harvest.

Yes, God has promised that men will pour into your bosom, pressed down, shaken together, and running over (Luke 6:38). But God wants you to be one of those who pour! Let your attitude be, "Lord, You can use me anytime You want to give someone else his harvest."

Harvest Comes
One Step at a Time

Let's look at Mark 4:28 again: **"The earth produces [acting] by itself—first the blade, then the ear, then the full grain in the ear."** What does that mean? This verse tells us harvest is a step-by-step progression. You're not usually going to see your entire harvest spring forth all at once.

If you were broke yesterday, chances are you probably won't wake up a millionaire tomorrow. It can happen, but most likely you will build toward that. If you were in debt yesterday, you may not get completely out of debt overnight. It took you a little time to get yourself in debt, so you'll probably get out of debt one step at a time.

Think again about the farmer. He doesn't go out to look at the field he's planted and say, "Oh, my goodness, only a bunch of blades are showing out of the ground! That's nothing! This sowing business doesn't work!" The farmer knows, however, that the blade will soon grow into an ear and then the full grain in the ear!

Yet some people say, "I planted a hundred dollars in the Sunday morning offering, and then someone gave me a twenty-dollar bill after service. That harvest doesn't even cover my seed! Planting seed doesn't work!" But in reality, they're just seeing the "blade"—only the beginning of their harvest.

The truth is, blessings come into our lives all the time which we don't count as harvest but which actually make up a part of our harvest. Some blessings may just be the blade, not the full-grown grain.

So don't say that sowing doesn't work; you don't want to kill the rest of your harvest with your words! Instead of looking at the blade as your total harvest, look at it as a sign of more harvest to come. Be grateful for the little blessings, and start saying, "Hallelujah! My harvest is already on its way!"

The full harvest usually comes gradually, so enter the rest of faith. And keep reminding yourself the progression of the harvest: first the blade, then the ear, then the full grain in the ear.

Don't Waver!

What happens to those who get weary of waiting after they sow seed and see only the blade or the ear of the harvest? Because they don't see an immediate, full return on their giving when they desire, some start to waver: "It's almost the due date for my rent. I don't know if God is bringing in my harvest or not."

The moment a person starts wavering, he cancels out his harvest:

> **...The one who wavers (hesitates, doubts) is like the billowing surge out at sea that is blown hither and thither and tossed by the wind.**
> **For truly, let not such a person imagine that he will receive anything [he asks for] from the Lord.**
> —James 1:6,7

The reason so many Christians don't receive what they need from God is that they waver back and forth in doubt and unbelief. On Sunday morning they say, "That sermon encouraged my faith. I believe my harvest is coming!" But on Monday night, they say, "Oh, what a terrible day at work! Lord, why doesn't this harvest come? I'm always broke. It's probably never going to come!"

No wonder those people do a lot of sowing and very little harvesting! They won't receive anything from God if they keep talking like that.

It's also important to realize that some harvests take longer than others because God moves through men. In other words, if the person God originally wanted to use as a channel of His provision for you isn't obedient to sow, He goes to plan B. Nevertheless, *you* will always reap in due season.

God isn't worried if plan A falls through, because He knows how to get your harvest to you. Meanwhile, the person who actually suffers is not you but the one who didn't obey the Holy Spirit's leading initially. He won't receive any harvest because he failed to sow.

I know a man who is both a minister and a musician, who can attest to the fact that you can slow down your harvest if you're not sensitive to sow according to the Lord's leading. This man was holding a meeting at a church one day when the Lord spoke to his spirit, saying, "Do you see that lady in the second row, third in from the aisle?"

"Yes, Lord," he answered.

"She's been believing Me for a piano a long time. You own a baby grand piano; I want you to give it to her."

"But, Lord, I'm a musician! I need the piano. I love to play it; it's a big part of my life and ministry!"

The Lord replied, "Oh? When did you get so attached to that piano?"

The minister got the message. "I understand, Lord," he said, and he walked over to the woman and told her he had a piano to give her. This, of course, blessed the woman beyond words.

After sowing his piano, this music minister began to believe God for a white grand piano to replace it.

Time went by, but no piano showed up. Finally, a year later the minister returned to the same church where he had given his piano away. After the service a woman came up to him and said, "I think I have a piano that belongs to you."

"What do you mean?" the man asked.

"Well, the Lord has really been dealing with me for some time now to give you my white grand piano."

"Hallelujah, glory to Jesus!" the man exclaimed. "By the way, when did God tell you this?"

"About a year ago," the woman replied, "the last time you were here."

And we wonder why our harvest is a little slow at times!

God moves around possessions and money among His people. As I've said several times, one person's seed is another's harvest. God gives a particular person several opportunities to sow according to His leading simply because He wants to get more harvest to that person.

But God won't wait forever. If the person won't obey His leading to give, God will eventually say, "I'm sorry, I can't wait on you anymore. You're not willing to be obedient, so I'll ask someone else to sow in this situation, and the harvest will go to the next person instead of you."

Catch the Spirit of Giving

The spirit of giving is available to all who receive it. Remember what Jesus said regarding the widow He watched throw only two mites into the treasury: "She gave of her want, therefore she will be blessed more than all those people who gave of their abundance." (Mark 12:42-44.) That woman had definitely caught the spirit of giving!

I know a modern-day example of that story. A man named Andrew from Nigeria volunteers in our ministry. He and his wife attend a Tulsa Bible school and have two children.

Andrew's father severely persecuted him after Andrew made the decision to give up his medical profession in Nigeria and attend a Bible training school in order to serve the Lord in full-time ministry. In fact, when Andrew returned to Nigeria the summer after his first year as a student, his father made sure Andrew was unable to obtain a new visa to return to the United States. Therefore, Andrew couldn't work in the United States when he returned that fall for his last year at school.

So during his second year of Bible school, Andrew and his family lived completely by faith. Finally, in December, Andrew was down to his last two dollars. He prayed, "Lord, I'm going to buy bread with one dollar and give You the other dollar. I'm trusting You to provide for me."

That next Monday evening, Andrew served as an usher at the Wisdom class I teach. When the offering plates were passed around, he put in his last dollar. Why? He did it in obedience to God.

(Let me tell you something about God. You never have to ask Him, "Should I give in this offering or not?" Giving or not giving is not an issue—the only issue is "How much?" And be careful when you ask God that question. His amount is almost always higher than the amount you thought it should be, because He wants to stretch your faith!)

As Andrew returned home after the Wisdom class that night, he didn't have a penny to his name. But at four o'clock in the morning, the telephone rang. It was a pastor in Nigeria.

"Andrew," the pastor said, "the Lord woke me up last night and told me to call and tell you I'm sending you one thousand U.S. dollars."

The next day at school, a classmate came up to Andrew and slipped a two-hundred dollar check into his hand.

After classes that day, Andrew approached the dean of the school and said, "Dean, I know I owe you for both my wife's and my tuition for last month and this month. I have to tell you that I don't have the money to pay you right now and if you want us to drop out, we will."

The dean replied, "I don't know what you're talking about. Your tuition is paid up for last month, this month, *and* next month! Someone walked in here and paid it for you and your wife!"

When Andrew arrived home that night, he got a call from an old friend in England. His friend told him, "Andrew, I'm sending you a check for two hundred dollars."

Before that week was over, Andrew had received a total of twenty-five hundred dollars! But God didn't stop there!

This all happened a few days before Christmas. The day after the call from England, the church gave Andrew a hamper full of Christmas food, and that night someone showed up at his apartment with a Christmas tree and decorations.

During the weeks preceding this financial breakthrough, Andrew's little daughter had asked him over and over, "Daddy, when is Santa going to bring Christmas presents?"

How was Andrew supposed to answer that question with only one dollar in his pocket? He kept saying, "Just believe God, Sweetheart. He will take care of us."

So his little girl believed God for a battery-operated toy Singer sewing machine. Then the night before Christmas, someone came to the family's apartment and dropped off eleven Christmas presents—one of them was a toy Singer sewing machine!

I've seen too many testimonies like Andrew's for anyone to convince me that God won't take care of His children. God is so good!

And how is Andrew today? He's doing great. Miracles continue to overtake him because he's still willing to trust God, even with his last dollar.

Andrew's story should inspire great faith to begin applying God's principles for financial increase in your life. It doesn't matter if you begin applying these principles, as I did, at a time in your life when your tithe check is thousands of dollars. It doesn't matter if, like Andrew, you give your last one.

What does matter? That God is faithful. He will meet you exactly where you are. He will rush toward you in the same way that the prodigal son's father rushed to him. He will help you. He will uphold you. And ultimately, He will bless you with the blessings of Abraham.

You'll be blessed coming in, and you'll be blessed going out. You will be blessed in everything you set your hand to do. Those enemies of poverty, lack and debt that have come against you in one direction will flee from you in seven directions.

Because He is Jehovah God, the Creator of heaven and earth. He watches jealously over His own Word to bring what He has spoken to pass. There is no investment banker or stock broker on earth who will do for you what He will do. Put your faith and trust in Him today.

Remember, it's up to our generation to accomplish what God has called us to do in these last days, and that is only possible through our knowledge of God's kingdom principles of financial success, and putting them into practice.

Therefore, don't grow weary as you wait in faith for your prosperity to manifest. Once you've done your part according to the Word, keep your faith stirred up and your mouth hooked up to your harvest. Think harvest, speak harvest, and praise God for your harvest.

No longer do you have to live in poverty and lack! As you get a revelation of these principles and begin living a lifestyle of sowing and reaping, the curse of poverty will be broken over your life. And as surely as God made day to follow night, your financial increase is on its way.

About the Author

Dr. Nasir K. Siddiki, a Muslim businessman in the 1980s, achieved phenomenal success by the world's standard. He had it all: money, power, status and a thriving business.

His life took a dramatic turn after a deadly virus attacked his nervous system. When physicians offered no hope, Nasir cried out to God. It was not Mohammed who answered his prayer. It was Jesus—the God of the Christians – who entered his hospital room and his life, leaving Nasir forever changed.

Nasir's first encounter with Jesus brought healing. His second encounter brought salvation. Finally, as Nasir studied the Bible with fervor, he encountered Jesus as his provider. When Nasir applied God's principles of financial increase his business exploded. Soon he was invited to speak at seminars where crowds of thousands arrived to learn his scriptural keys to success.

Today, Dr. Nasir Siddiki is dedicated to teaching those biblical principles to audiences worldwide through Bible colleges, universities, seminars, church services, and monthly teaching tapes. He has also taught Biblical Economics at the American Bible College and Seminary, where he was awarded an honorary doctorate for his work in this field.

Dr. Siddiki currently lives with his wife, Anita, and their three children in Tulsa, Oklahoma, where Wisdom Ministries is based.

Free Tape

For your FREE tape on miracles, a complete list of Dr. Nasir Siddiki's teaching materials, or ministry engagements, please contact us at:

Wisdom Ministries

P. O. Box 2720

Broken Arrow, Oklahoma 74013-2720

(918) 712-7122

www.wisdomministries.org

When you contact us, please include your praise reports if the principles presented in this book have helped you.

Tapes and CDs Available

Dr. Nasir Siddiki

Authority of the Believer - Vol 1
Authority of the Believer - Vol 2
Becoming a Spiritual Giant - Vol 1
Becoming a Spiritual Giant - Vol 2
Catching the Spirit of Excellence - Vol 1
Catching the Spirit of Excellence - Vol 2
Catching the Spirit of Excellence - Vol 3
Common Sense Trading Led By the Holy Spirit
Experiencing God's Glory
Explosive Power of the Word
Faith That Brings Victory
Favor with God & Man
Flying High in Business Vol 1
Flying High in Business Vol 2
For Men Only
God Is Faithful
God's Prerequisite of Wealth
Growing Up Spiritually
Harness the Power of Money
Healing Made Simple
How to Know the Voice of God
How to Receive the Commanded Blessing
Issues that Stop Your Healing
Kingdom Principles of Financial Increase
Leadership Principles - Vol 1
Leadership Principles - Vol 2
Leadership Principles - Vol 3
Life After Debt

Managing Money God's Way
Mark of a Winner
Offerings That God Must Multiply
People Skills God's Way
Prayer - The Currency of the Kingdom
Prayer That Moves Angels
Prosperity - Motives of the Heart
Rest of Faith
Secrets of Successful Prayer
Strongholds of the Mind - Vol 1
Strongholds of the Mind - Vol 2
Strongholds of the Mind - Vol 3
Strongholds of the Mind - Vol 4
Strongholds of the Mind - Vol 5
Strongholds of the Mind - Vol 6
Strongholds of the Mind - Vol 7
The Voice Of God
What Feeds the Seed
Winning On Wall Street - Vol 1
Winning On Wall Street - Vol 2
Wisdom for Business - Vol 1
Wisdom for Business - Vol 2
Wisdom for Successful Living
Worship - Drawing Near to God - Vol 1
Worship - Drawing Near to God - Vol 2
Worship - Entering the Holy of Holies - Vol 3

Anita Siddiki

Hearing the Voice of the Holy Spirit

Dr. Nasir & Anita Siddiki

Bridge to the Spiritual Realm
Marriage: God's Plan - Heaven on Earth - Vol 1
Marriage: Sizzling Sex God's Way - Vol 2
Marriage: Communication is the Key - Vol 3
Marriage: The Difference between Men &
                Women - Vol 4
Obtaining Your Healing

Manuals

Common Sense Trading Led By the Holy Spirit
Winning On Wall Street

Video

Dr. Nasir and Anita's Miracle Healing Testimony

For your **FREE** tape on miracles
Or
To **order**, please contact us at:
Wisdom Ministries P. O. Box 2720
Broken Arrow, OK 74013
(918) 712-7122
www.wisdomministries.org